MARCH OF THE HOOLIGANS

MARCH OF THE HOOLIGANS

SOCCER'S BLOODY FRATERNITY

Dougie Brimson

Distributed by Holtzbrinck Publishers

Designed by Jason Snyder

Library of Congress Cataloging-in-Publication Data

Brimson, Dougie, 1959-
  March of the hooligans : soccer's bloody fraternity / Dougie
Brimson. -- 1st ed.
    p. cm.
  Includes bibliographical references and index.
  ISBN-13: 978-0-7535-1293-7 (alk. paper)
  ISBN-10: 0-7535-1293-9 (alk. paper)
  1. Soccer hooliganism--Great Britain. 2. Soccer fans--Great Britain. 3.
Violence in sports--Great Britain. I. Title.
  GV943.9.F35B746 2007
  796.3340941--dc22

                        2007033397

ISBN-13: 978-0-7535-1293-7
ISBN-10: 0-7535-1293-9

10 9 8 7 6 5 4 3 2 1

*For my wife, Tina, who amazes
and inspires me every single day.*

CONTENTS

- -

ACKNOWLEDGMENTS

- -

With huge thanks to Alabama Paul, Tim Zaal, and Justin Hopper for their advice, Ken Siman for the opportunity, and Marc Haeringer for his patience and brilliant editing. I would also like to thank all at Headline (UK) for their help with permissions.

INTRODUCTION

I am, or at least I was, a soccer hooligan. I say "was" because I moved on. I went from fighting to writing largely because I'd become mystified as to how something that had become such an integral yet damaging part of England's soccer culture continued to be so obviously misunderstood by those who were not a part of it. I was also sick of going to matches and watching my back all the time, wondering if the next game I went to would see me or someone I knew get badly beaten or worse.

So I decided that instead of being a part of the problem I would try to explain exactly what hooliganism is all about, and why for decades it has posed such a huge danger to the global game of soccer. I have done that by writing and talking about my own life as both a soccer fan and a hooligan, everything from how I got involved in violence at games and the things I did to the incident that tipped me over the edge and made me decide to get out.

It is fair to say that this hasn't won me many friends. The authorities here in England quickly came to regard me as a thorn in their side, and a number of active hooligans, including many friends, accused me of selling out. There were even occasions where I had to fight my way out of bars or soccer grounds, so angry were people who I had once counted as mates. There are also plenty with whom my own experiences strike a chord. As a consequence, I've written thirteen books, have been published around the world, and have even written a couple of movies. The most notable of these is the award-winning *Green Street Hooligans*, which starred everyone's favorite hobbit Elijah Wood.

For some time now I have been keeping a wary eye on the growing soccer scene in the US. The team LA Galaxy's purchase of the great David Beckham is undoubtedly going to provide the game with a huge boost, and I have a very real concern that he isn't the only English import that is going to influence American soccer over the coming seasons. Indeed, I will be amazed if within a couple of years the game in the US has not become infected with at least some symptoms of the so-called English disease.

You guys certainly don't have to sit back and wait for it to happen in the belief that such a thing is inevitable because, believe me, it isn't. If you have the balls to stand up and be counted, hooliganism can certainly be stopped in its tracks.

The sad thing is that from what I have seen, that isn't likely because most people in the US have little or no real idea of what hooliganism is all about. Oh, the American comedian Bill Hicks might once have ridiculed it as being "quaintly English" and it might look random and stupid on TV but trust me, hooliganism isn't anything like that. It's organized, ritualized, violent, and very dangerous. Why else do you think the game is forced to pour millions into anti-hooligan security whenever and wherever a major tournament is staged?

For those who are or have been actively involved, the culture of hooliganism and soccer violence is exciting and addictive, but most important, it is huge fun. It's what they do. It's the culture that soccer has become for them and something that they will never give up. Why would they? It is vital that the American public begins to learn what goes on among the hooligan fraternity and why. For only by doing so can you ever hope to understand what may to happen to your game. If hooliganism takes hold of the game in America, it will happen for one reason and one reason only: because no one bothered to try and stop it.

Before we get engrossed in all of that, it is important to understand something. You see, I am English, not American, and as a wise man once said, we are two nations divided by a common language. To be more specific, I'm a Londoner, which means that slang is an integral element in the way I speak. It is also an integral part of the way I write, so it will undoubtedly prove useful for you if I provide an explanation of some of the terms that soccer fans here use when we talk about the greatest of games.

Apologies if some of them offend but, if they do, too bad.

GLOSSARY

Adidas: Makers of the world's greatest training shoes. Obligatory wear for any self-respecting soccer fan.

aggro: Violent behavior, as in "They were looking for aggro!"

anorak: A person who watches a game bedecked in team jerseys, scarves, and stupid hats. Usually children, old men, geeks, nerds, or women.

armchair: A person who watches his soccer on TV rather than actually bothering to go watch a game live. Invariably follows one of the larger more successful teams such as Manchester United or Liverpool, as these feature on TV the most.

Arsenal: North London soccer club. One of the greatest of all the English sides even though their team is currently managed by a Frenchman, consists entirely of foreign players, and is owned by an American billionaire.

barmies: Soccer fans who occasionally cause problems at games. Best thought of as second-string hooligans.

barmy: Crazy.

Beckham, David: Soccer-playing god. Former England national captain who is possibly one of the greatest dead-ball kickers the game has ever seen. Blessed with good looks, huge amounts of money, and a decent-looking wife, it now appears he is destined for a career in Hollywood.

blag: To obtain something for nothing, as in "I blagged a free ticket."

bollocks: A favored word among soccer fans because of the fact that it can have many different and useful meanings. For example: "This beer is the bollocks" (That's a very good beer, landlord) or "That's bollocks" (You're talking rubbish, officer). Can also be used as "I was bollocksed" (I was very drunk).

bottle: Slang word for courage, as in "he's got bottle" or "that takes some bottle." A coward is known as a "bottler."

Burberry: Designer label once favored by Casuals (see definition below). The brand is well past its sell-by date and desperate to distance itself from soccer, anyway.

buzz (the): The adrenaline rush that comes from being involved with hooliganism. The feeling is as addictive a drug as crack, and just as difficult to give up.

Cardiff City: Welsh soccer club that somehow manages to play in the English soccer league. Better known for its notorious hooligan following than for the quality of their soccer, which is generally piss poor.

Casual: The youth cult that grew out of soccer in England during the late 1970s and early 1980s, known for their expensive designer clothes and trainers (shoes), which formed a type of uniform. The Casuals are at the heart of the whole hooligan issue. They're still around, still going strong, and still looking the bollocks.

Chelsea: West London soccer club owned by a Russian billionaire, and currently coached by a Portuguese egomaniac. Widely accused of buying its way to numerous trophies in recent years, hated with a vengeance by just about everyone outside West London. Chelsea fans have been at the forefront of the hooligan problem since the 1970s.

crew: Slang term for a group of hooligans allied to a particular club. Most have nicknames that over the years have become synonymous with the club they follow. For example: the Inter City Firm (West Ham United), Zulu Army (Birmingham City), and 657 Crew (Portsmouth FC). Also known as firms or mobs.

Derby: A game between local rival teams. The most important games of the year, these matches aren't simply about soccer; they are about bragging rights over any lads you know, and even members of your own family. For that reason, the results of the games are fiercely contested both on and off the playing field. Also the name of an English soccer club (Derby County).

diamond: Very good, as in "He's a diamond geezer."

end: The terraces behind the goals. The home ends were where the local lads stood and were prime targets for attack from visiting hooligans back in the 1970s and 1980s and thus would be fiercely defended. These were where reputations were made and lost.

FA: The Football Association. The governing body of the game in England.

FIFA: Governing body of world soccer.

fixture list: The dates of all the games in a season. This is the calendar around which all non–soccer related events, such as weddings, must be planned.

football: What the rest of the world calls soccer. Often shortened to footie.

France: Bastard nation on the other side of the English Channel to us. Rolled over without a murmur when Hitler turned up in 1939.

geezer: Differs from the American definition (an old man) in that in an English sense a geezer is a positive expression for someone who exudes self-confidence ("He's a bit of a geezer"). Can also be used as a term of respect ("He's a top geezer").

geezer-bird: A woman who tries to act like a man. Or a butch lesbian.

Germany: Bastard nation that always seems to beat the English when it matters (except for 1918, 1945, and 1966, although only one of those was at soccer).

Glasgow Celtic: Scottish soccer club most famous for its hatred of Glasgow Rangers and everything English.

Glasgow Rangers: Scottish soccer club most famous for its hatred of Glasgow Celtic and everything English.

grass: To inform on someone. Not good.

ground: Another word for stadium.

hot dog: The most beautiful-smelling food item ever created by man. Unlike the American version, however, in England these are usually sold outside soccer grounds by people of dubious hygiene. Avoid like the plague unless you have a liking for stadium toilets or are very drunk.

Italy: European nation where everything decent ends in a vowel (pizza, Armani, Ferrari, and footie) and the setting for the greatest World Cup tournament ever staged (Italia '90). Also home to some of the most crazed hooligan gangs in world soccer.

Lacoste: Favored designer label of Casuals and geezers everywhere. Will never go out of vogue, ever.

lads: Similar to geezer as a positive expression for a group of males. For example, "I'm off out with the lads" (I am going for a drink with my friends, my darling) or "That's a handy group of lads" (That's a group of men to be avoided).

lash: To drink heavily, as in "We're out on the lash."

leg over: Refreshment of the horizontal kind, as in "I got my leg over that blonde last night."

lesbian: See geezer-bird or women's soccer.

Liverpool: One of the most famous soccer clubs in world football. Supported by people known as Scousers for reasons best known to themselves. Now owned by two very wealthy Americans.

Luton Town: Small, inconsequential soccer club that is the local rival to my own club, the glorious Watford FC. Also known as "Shit Town" or "The Scum." The official club nickname is "The Hatters," which is also Cockney rhyming slang for homosexual (Brown Hatter). That says it all, really.

Manchester United: Probably the most famous soccer club on the planet and supported by legions of armchairs, the vast majority of whom would never even dream of traveling to Manchester from where they live in Hong Kong or Johannesburg to see them play. Currently owned by an American businessman.

Millwall: Probably the most infamous soccer club on the planet due to its notorious hooligan following that, at one point, seemed to make up 100 percent of their support. All Millwall fans should be regarded as geezers, even the women.

missile: Anything that is thrown, be it a coin, brick, or even a dart.

MLS: Major League Soccer. The money men, I mean driving force, behind soccer in the US.

mob: A collective noun for a group of hooligans, as in "That is some mob." Can also be used in a collective sense, as in "We were well mobbed up." See also firm or crew.

mug: A term used to describe someone who is stupid, as in "He's a mug."

OB: The Old Bill or police.

off: Slang term meaning a fight or disagreement of some kind and used as "It's going off," "It went off," "It kicked off," or "There's been an off." Can also mean a player being sent off the field of play, in which case it will be accompanied by the crowd shouting "off, off, off." Also, a way of telling someone you are leaving a location quickly ("I'm doing the off").

pitch: The playing field.

police: Known universally as "Old Bill" or "The Filth." The sworn enemy of lads everywhere, as their primary role is to spoil the fun. However, they are handy to have around if things look like they are going to turn nasty.

ponce: The practice of borrowing without any intention of repayment, as in "poncing." Not good and rightly frowned upon.

premier league: Known universally as the Premiership. The pinnacle of the English game and widely regarded as the greatest league in world soccer. This is where the money is.

ran: Slang term meaning to chase, as in "We ran them." Can also simply mean to run away ("We ran like fuck!").

replica kit: Copies of team jerseys sold as a cynical ploy to relieve supporters of hard-earned money. Should never be worn by anyone who thinks of themselves as a Casual. Ever.

Saturday scene: Blanket term to describe the match day experience.

Scottish soccer: Piss-poor imitation of soccer in England, which is where most of the teams in Scotland would be playing if they were given half a chance.

scum: Term for local rivals. Their fans are universally known as scummers.

shoeing: A beating.

slag: To criticize, as in "to slag off." Can also mean a female of dubious moral standards ("She's a right old slag").

snide: Fake or false.

soccer: What you Americans call the sport known the world over as football. Not to be confused with American football, a very odd game indeed.

specials: Trains used to ferry supporters to and from games back in the 1970s and 1980s. They were fantastic fun to be on as most of the journey would be spent fighting with other lads, throwing things out of the windows, and destroying the carriages. The railways stopped running them. Can't imagine why.

stand: The grandstands that surround playing fields, as in "We sat in the stands."

steam: To run as a group, as in "We steamed after them."

Stone Island: Designer label that for a time was the label of choice for Casuals. Now out of vogue because of its copious forgeries, failing quality, and the fact that the mere sight of the logo is enough to convince the police that you are guilty of something.

suss: To figure out what someone's up to, as in "We've got you sussed."

swerve: To avoid, as in "Give those lads the swerve."

take the piss: To mock, take liberties, or dish out a beating, as in "We took the piss big time."

terrace: Area where soccer fans used to stand inside stadia. Usually situated behind a goal and fiercely defended against rival/visiting supporters who shouldn't be there anyway. Terraces have largely been replaced by seated areas in the continuing drive to attract a new audience to the sport, which has destroyed the traditionally hostile atmosphere at many English grounds. While some may argue this is a good thing, to those of us who were around in the 1970s and 1980s it is the exact opposite.

terrace grapevine: The rumor mill through which news of hooligan activities is spread. Used to revolve around pubs, train stations, and freeway rest stops, which meant that news took ages to filter out. Now replaced by the Internet.

toes: To run, as in "We were on our toes" or "They're on their toes."

top boy: The leader of a group of fans, as in "He's their top boy."

top man: A good guy, as in "He's a top man."

turn over: To score a victory over someone or something, as in "We turned them over."

UEFA: Governing body of European soccer.

Watford: The team I support because it is the professional club nearest to my hometown (and any fan worth his salt should support his local side). Known as the "Golden Boys" or the "Hornets" on account of the team colors of yellow and black. Most famous for once being owned by Elton John and for the battle cry, "Come on you 'Orns!"

West Ham United: The pride of East London and one of the few clubs whose support is almost entirely made up of geezers. Their stadium is not a place to visit if you are of a nervous disposition.

women's soccer: In many Englishmen's opinion, women and soccer should be kept apart at all times. I have a degree of empathy with that.

wrong'un: Someone who is of dodgy morals, as in "He's a wrong 'un."

Yanks: Americans. Also known as "spams."

Zulu Army: One of the most notorious hooligan groups in English soccer. Not to be messed with.

CHAPTER ONE

Me, Myself, and I

You don't know the half of it.

I'm in a strange city walking back to my car with my brother and two mates after watching our beloved Watford dish out a 4–0 spanking to the local soccer team. We're keeping our heads down because the rival club's supporters have a reputation for being less than welcoming toward visiting fans.

Suddenly, coming toward us are about fifteen lads. We know instantly that they're soccer lads because they're all wearing the typical hooligan uniform of designer labels and arrogance. We don't recognize them and they look seriously pissed, which means only one thing; they are local lads.

As we pass, they eyeball us angrily but carry on walking. Just as we think we've gotten away with it, we hear one of them say "cockney cunts." We know we're in trouble. We quicken our pace but it's too late. The sound of running is all the incentive we need to break into a sprint that would have had Carl Lewis struggling to keep up. It isn't enough.

We split up and head in different directions toward the car park where the sanctuary of my Alfa Romeo is waiting for me. The bulk of the lads seem to realize that I'm older than the other three, and that I've spent years existing on a diet of lager and Marlboros, so they come after me. A wise move on their part, as the distance between us begins to shrink rapidly.

By now I'm actually in the car park, but I realize that there is no escape. All I can do is stop and face the locals before they catch me. Within seconds, I'm alone and surrounded. A quick glance around and I can see cars full of fellow Watford fans, but they are all families, not a single lad to be seen. The sound of the door-lock buttons going down is almost deafening. "Bollocks," I think. "This is it."

I search around for the leader—there's always a leader—and this time he stands out because of the bloody great lump of wood he has in his hand. "Well, Cockney, where do you want this?"

Straight away, his voice and his tone piss me off, but good sense prevails. By now I've also noticed the nail sticking out of the plank he's holding. "Look, mate, I don't want any trouble."

"Too bad, it's here, boy," he says. I quickly look around to see that not only are his mates ready for it but I now have carloads of soccer fans hoping they are about to see some-one get a good kicking just to round off their day.

My mind is racing but there's really only one thing I can do. If I'm going to get a kicking, this bastard in front of me is going to catch at least one, and the biggest one, I can get in. "Come on then, you cunt," I scream. "Let's fucking go!"

I start to run forward, suddenly aware that his mates have stepped back, stunned, and that he's just standing there staring at me. It suddenly occurs to me that I might be able to slap him once and get past and away before they know what is happening. Then I would at least have me a chance. But before I can move any farther, he realizes what's going on, steps to one side, and smashes the wood across the side of my leg. The nail sinks cleanly into my thigh. I drop like a stone, curling into a ball before I hit the ground so that the expected kicking will do as little damage as possible.

I'm lying there, waiting for it to start, and someone screams, "Leave him, get the other bastards!" and they van-ish. I can't believe it. I just lay there for a couple of seconds and then sit up. They've gone. Thank Christ for that.

I pull the wood, nail still attached, out of my thigh, and with a curse, I stand up and stagger over to my car. My leg is killing me, but that's nothing compared to the heady mixture of relief, anger, and shame that is coursing through my veins. No one likes taking a beating, especially not in public.

Then, as I'm lighting a Marlboro, I hear a noise. They're back for round two. Only this time it's worse because my car is at risk as well, a fact confirmed by the various lumps of brick they are holding.

The leader steps forward again. "Well, well, look who's 'ere."

"Okay, mate, fair enough." I try to sound convincing but I'm bloody terrified. "But please, not the motor."

He stands there looking at me and the blokes with him start to shout. It's coming again at any moment, or so I think.

"Leave 'im, he's had enough."

I look at him, relief coursing through me. "Thanks, mate, thanks a lot."

He steps forward, and with a jab into my chest he retorts, "I'm not your fuckin' mate, right?" Then they turn and walk away, hurling abuse at anyone within hearing distance.

This is no work of fiction; it happened to me a few years ago. While such an assault would have had any sane person heading for the local police station, the very thought never even entered my head. You see, this wasn't an assault, it was an "off."

You know about hooliganism, right? Hooligans are those guys you see every so often on CNN and NBC fighting with one another inside and outside soccer stadiums across Europe and South America. Yeah, well, that was me. I was one of those guys, and for me and the many thousands of guys like me such events were an occupational hazard. If you dished it out, once in a while you'd have to be prepared to take it.

Those who know little or nothing about hooliganism, and that includes the majority of politicians and journalists, would like to believe that anyone involved in the culture of soccer violence is a brain-dead, cave-dwelling moron who, if not the product of a broken home, is certainly the result of an unstable upbringing.

The truth is somewhat different. Over the years I have met many hundreds of people involved in hooliganism, and with very few exceptions, they are decent, friendly, and above all normal lads. All this may seem hard to swallow given the fact that they are involved in what is after all, violent, organized, criminal activity, but it is nevertheless a fact.

Indeed, I am constantly amazed by the types of people I meet who are or have been involved in hooliganism: doctors, lawyers, bankers, factory workers, journalists, policemen, firemen, actors, company directors, taxi drivers, etc. You name it. There are even numerous instances of celebrities being involved with firms—groups of hooligans—including one very well known English pop star who has allegedly not only been involved with a particular firm but also has occasionally funded their activities.

But almost to a man the very idea of throwing a chair, a

brick, or even a punch at anyone on a normal day would have almost all of them scratching their heads in astonishment. At soccer, however, things are different. People routinely behave in a way that is totally at odds with their day-to-day lives.

If you actually bother to ask hooligans why they became hooligans, something most people who "study" this issue seem somewhat reluctant to do, many will simply shrug their shoulders, others will say, "It's the buzz," while a few will simply say, "Why not?" None of which, of course, provides anything approaching an answer. If you step back and think about it though, this is a question that is being asked ass-backwards. The truth is that, in most cases, people do not adopt the culture of hooliganism; it adopts them. You do not suddenly decide that going to soccer and causing trouble would be a good idea; either you go to soccer first and it gradually sucks you in until you have become a part of the problem without even realizing or even acknowledging it or, in my case, you actually let yourself be drawn into it because it's what you want to do.

My earliest recollection of soccer as a professional sport probably dates back to 1964. My dad, being a postwar refugee from North London, was a Tottenham Hotspurs fan. I can vividly remember standing in the garden of my grandparents' house listening to the noise of the crowd coming from their stadium at White Hart Lane one Saturday afternoon. Despite agonizing pleas, my father never took me to see them play. This was a serious error of judgment on his part because I rebelled and followed another club, Watford.

Ironically, the one and only game to which he ever took me was a Watford game. I have no idea why we went, but I was about nine years old and the Golden Boys (the Watford team) were playing Bristol Rovers. It was, I recall, a 1–0 win for Watford, but all I really remember was that the stadium was half-empty, it was freezing cold that day, and the game was boring. I avoided soccer for a while after that, other than playing it, of course, and settled into life as a Speedway and stock car racing fan. However, that all changed in 1970 when I sat down to watch the Football Association (FA) cup final at Wembley. It was one of the greatest games of all time but, more important, I discovered my first sporting hero, a player called Peter Osgood. His headed goal in that game remains one of the best I have ever seen, and I knew that one day I would have to visit Stamford Bridge in West London to see him play for Chelsea, and one day I did.

A couple of years later, alone and shit-scared, I sneaked out of the house, jumped on a train, and headed for London. I did not, however, make it to Stamford Bridge that day because as I stepped out of the subway station on the way to the stadium a fight broke out. Not any old fight either, but a mass, full-bore soccer brawl.

To a fresh-faced youth of thirteen, the sight of hundreds of lads trying to beat the shit out of one another while a few policemen tried in vain to keep them apart was something of a shock. I'd heard about hooligans, of course, and seen bits in the papers, but this was the real deal and it was going on right in front of me. There were guys lying on the floor bleeding while others were punching and kicking anything that moved. Others just seemed to be doing nothing but running around but it all added to the spectacle. And the soundtrack: a wall of noise made up of shouting and chanting. It was bloody fantastic.

I must admit that, in spite of my excitement, I shit myself good and proper. As soon as the trouble died down I was out of there. I didn't even go to the game because it suddenly struck me that if it was like this outside the stadium before the game, what was it going to be like afterward?

The trouble made the newspapers the following day, and not only did I devour every word but I let all my mates know that I'd been there and seen it all for real. My match day program and train ticket stub were all the proof I needed to back up my slightly distorted version of events. Well, I could hardly tell anyone I had bottled it, could I?

The more I told the story, the more I expanded events until, in the end, even I got sick of talking about it. But by then I was hooked. I'd had my first taste of the "buzz," and watching soccer would never be the same again.

Anyone who has experienced the buzz knows that no matter how that first fix happens, once it has hold of you that's it. So addictive does this rush become that it is very difficult to pull back. I've fought in two wars, flown in fighter jets, raced cars and motorbikes, and done all kinds of other amazing things in my life, but being involved in soccer violence is without doubt the most incredibly exciting and enjoyable thing I have ever known. A statement that to anyone who has not been a part of it will sound astonishing but it is, nevertheless, the truth.

Nothing else allows you the opportunity to experience every emotion known to man within the space of ten minutes on occasion. I have argued that soccer hooliganism is the original extreme sport, and I have never met anyone able to convince me otherwise. Let's face it, if so called sports such as snowboarding and bungee-jumping are about placing yourself at risk and overcoming your fears to experience elation and relief, it doesn't take a genius to work out that exactly the same thing applies to hooliganism. You cannot tell me that hurtling down a slippery slope on a plank of polished wood could possibly get the adrenaline pumping more vigorously than walking though the side streets of a provincial English town with ten or twenty mates on a match day. It really does get the senses buzzing.

While the reasons people go snowboarding or do hooliganism can be legitimately compared, being involved in soccer violence actually has one distinct advantage if you are looking for excitement. You see, once you've hurtled down that slope on your plank a few times, the rush you get from it diminishes, and you're off looking for a longer and more slippery slope. For the hooligans, however, every match day is different from the last because each corner you turn could be *the* corner. You might not even have any kind of fight, you might be simply running away from someone else, but however it happens the adrenaline levels rise and the heart rate goes through the roof — in other words, a massive and addictive rush.

Within a few months of my fateful first visit to Stamford Bridge, I met a lad from my school who had also fallen in love with Chelsea. We became almost regulars on what remains one of the most infamous soccer ends of all time, the Shed. This was a sprawling concrete terrace where thousands of the most loyal, vocal, and violent Chelsea supporters stood at each and every home game. Among them were me and my mate. We stood as far from the hard-core hooligans who inhabited the space directly behind the goal as was possible, yet we were still close enough to think of ourselves as being a part of it all.

Inevitably, we soon adopted the standard hooligan habit of scanning the crowd for any sign of invaders and joining in the pushing and shoving. It was awesome! And that was just inside the stadium. Outside was more often than not total mayhem. It seemed that every time we'd go, something would happen to scare the shit out of us, but as soon as we could the two of us would be back for more. The problem was the more often we went, the braver we got, and eventually we ended up standing almost, but not quite, behind the goal and right next to the hard-core lads.

One Saturday afternoon I was standing there minding my own business when a full-bore riot began right in front of me. Lads fought with chains, clubs, the lot, and eventually the police sent the dogs in. Even that didn't stop them, though, and in the end some of them began waving knives around within inches of us. For my mate, that was it. It was too scary. Although I went back on my own once after that and was chased around Euston Railway Station by some Arsenal fans, I stopped going to Stamford Bridge after that. I still missed soccer on Saturday afternoons, though, and since a few of my schoolmates were fans of our local club, I decided to accept their invitation and visit Vicarage Road to watch Watford. Although not the same, it quickly became a regular habit.

Although hooliganism was a major and increasing problem for the game in England at that time, it was something we rarely saw in those days at "The Vic," as we called our home stadium, Vicarage Road, primarily because Watford was languishing in the lower depths of the league. Indeed, to be honest, I can't recall a single incident of trouble from those times other than the odd exchange of curses. But largely thanks to the tabloid press, which even back then were fascinated with the subject of hooliganism, I was able to keep my eye on events in West London and elsewhere.

Things changed dramatically for me when, at the end of 1975, as a mere seventeen-year-old, I left home and joined the Royal Air Force. I soon found myself far from everything I knew studying the intricacies of aircraft hydraulics and keeping the Soviet Union at bay. I also found myself in the company of lads from all over the UK, the majority of whom were soccer fans. Although we would make the odd trip to see a local game it was never the same as watching our own teams. I certainly missed Watford and my mates. Thankfully, at the end of 1976, I was posted to a base just twelve miles from my home. I rapidly returned to the fray, and although it was clear to just about every soccer fan in the land that hooliganism was becoming an increasing problem, it was alarming to discover that it had even taken hold at Watford.

Each week it seemed that in spite of the team's lowly position in the league, violence both inside and outside the field was becoming commonplace. Thankfully, I had the good sense to realize that as a member of Her Majesty's Armed Forces I had a duty to maintain a discreet distance from any trouble, mostly due to the fear that I would be thrown into a military stockade if I were ever arrested. If I did find myself anywhere near trouble I was out of there.

Very occasionally, however, trouble was unavoidable. As any male knows, the power your pals can exert over you is immense. Indeed, it is easy to tell someone that he should walk away from trouble if it breaks out, but that isn't so simple for him to do if he's with a group of lads. After all, for most of us, one of the main appeals of going to soccer in the first place is that it is very much a group activity. Let's face it, if you go to a game on your own and start mouthing off, pretty soon you'll be either under arrest or under anesthetic. But if you're with a group of lads such behavior is more often than not expected of you.

One such incident involved West Ham United when the team its their first-ever league visit to our stadium in 1979. With a large hooligan following that had one of the worst reputations of any club in the land, they would be keen to let us know who was boss, we knew. For reasons that had nothing to do with soccer but were instead rooted in the fact that I was a horny bastard tempted by the promise of a bout of horizontal refreshment, I'd taken a girl to the game. My mate John who, like me, was well versed in the ways of the soccer terrace as well as all things skirt-related, also brought a date.

Within seconds of taking our usual place on the Watford terrace, we realized that we were surrounded by lads who neither of us had ever seen before and, inevitably, the second the teams appeared on the pitch it all kicked off. Not just around us but in just about every single section of the 20,000-plus crowd. Since neither female had ever attended a game before, the sight of grown men fighting all around them was something of an eye opener, and it was not helped by the fact that their two dates were apparently busily joining in. Romantic it was not. I did get my leg over, though, which was something.

Another incident took place on the visitors' terraces at Queens Park Rangers (QPR) at a game that didn't even involve Watford at all. For reasons that are buried in my memory, I joined a carload of fellow servicemen and headed for East London to watch West Ham United. Unfortunately, the car broke down on the way and by, the time we had fixed it, the only game we could make before kickoff time was QPR versus Liverpool in West London. As one of our number was a Liverpool fan and I have a deep-rooted dislike of QPR—a legacy of my one and only away trip with Chelsea—we decided to go in with the Liverpool supporters. We were to regret the decision almost instantly. One of the lads we had with us was black and, although no one said anything to him directly, it was clear that his presence had been noted and was unwelcome. At halftime we went to the toilet together. As we came out, he was suddenly surrounded by a group of young kids, none of whom looked to be older than ten years old, who demanded money. His response was immediate and to the negative but they persisted and began shoving the two of us. I may be a fat slob these days, but back then I was fit as fuck, and the lad who with me was heavily into weight training and, as a result, built like a brick shithouse. A few swift clouts and the little fuckers vanished only to be immediately replaced by decidedly bigger fuckers. Amazingly, we managed to fight our way out and dived over the barriers and onto the pitch before being escorted round to the home end. It was desperate—and decidedly scary—stuff.

The next occasion came only a few weeks later when I became involved in a bizarre incident with some Fulham fans in a graveyard in the center of Watford. I was walking back to my car after the game, taking a shortcut across the tombstones, when this little mob of visiting hooligans appeared from nowhere and began hitting out at anyone they could reach. I was on the far side of the graveyard from them and, seeing this, began moving away. When I saw one of them hit an old man and knock him down, however, I saw red and steamed across. By the time the police arrived, I had the old guy's attacker on the ground with his arm up his back, but the police grabbed me and tried to haul me away, leaving the real attacker free to walk off. Thankfully, with a flash of my military ID card—a tool that was to become increasingly useful as time passed—I was released and sent on my way.

In the early 1980s, as my military career and a posting to Germany took over, my involvement with English soccer petered out for a while. When I was home on leave, I attended as many games as I could. I was posted back to England from Germany at the beginning of 1982, a year in which a number of things happened that were to have a major effect not just on the way I followed soccer but on my entire life.

The first of these is that when I came back from Germany, it was to a base in Oxfordshire, just forty miles from my home. As luck would have it, the camp already had a resident contingent of Watford fans and so I, now twenty-three years old, immediately became a part of the match day exodus to Vicarage Road. The second thing that happened was that in April Argentina invaded the Falkland Islands. As an expert in aircraft crash recovery with recent frontline fighter experience, I was immediately put on twenty-four-hour stand-by to go. The third and most important thing was that I caught the back end of one of the great seasons in Watford's history. Funded by Elton John, our coach Graham Taylor had got the team working as a fantastic unit. Although none of us knew it, we were on the verge of the greatest era the club would ever see.

The team had already secured promotion to the first division (what we now call the Premiership) and so the plan was for the last two games of the season to be nothing more than a party. Our last home game at Vicarage Road was just that. I can't remember that much about it, although I do know I ended up dancing in one of the town fountains. Not a good idea when you have an hour's drive to get home and no change of clothes!

The final game of the season, however, was a different thing entirely. Watford faced an away trip to Derby County, and Derby needed to beat us to avoid relegation to the third division. It didn't take a genius to work out that the mood at Derby's home stadium, the Baseball Ground, was going to be, to say the least, hostile.

For the first time, at least the first time I had seen, Watford took a serious mob to an away game and things quickly turned nasty. Not because of the Derby supporters but because of the local police who were what I can only describe as a shameful example of their profession. On the walk from the train station to the Ground, they were at best rude and, at worst, abusive. I might well be a wanker but I certainly don't take kindly to a policeman calling me a wanker, nor do I want to see people being pushed along like cattle or dragged out of crowds and threatened with arrest for doing nothing more than singing.

Once they got us inside they even became violent. Watford supporters were verbally and physically abused, fingers poked through fences were hit with truncheons, and as the police walked along the perimeter of the pitch they repeatedly kicked stones into the faces of the people in the packed visitor's enclosure. When halftime came, the Watford contingent was almost rabid. Fences were pulled down and all sorts of things from coins to rocks were being hurled at the police and the Derby fans. And outside the stadium after the game, things just went ballistic. The worst incident of many involved a mounted policeman who was trying to stop us from attacking the Derby fans. As about 150 of us fought with some of his colleagues, his horse reared up and he fell off. He caught one of his feet in the stirrups, and as the animal tried to get away he was dragged along as the crowd kicked seven bells of shit out of him. It was a horrible thing to witness. Although a few Watford lads tried to help him, it was just too manic and it was only the intervention of another mounted policeman that rescued him. It is no exaggeration to say that the Watford fans caused mayhem that day and trouble carried on for hours. After many years following the Golden Boys, I have to say, even though I was right in the middle of it all, I was astonished that supporters of my club could do so much damage to both people and property.

I, however, had other concerns. Just three days later I was on a plane heading to the south Atlantic as a part of Maggie Thatcher's Task Force. Thankfully, the war with the Argentineans was not a long and drawn-out affair, and I was one of those fortunate enough to return home safe. If experiencing war teaches you one thing, it's that life is too short. Enjoy what you can, when you can. With this in mind, I put the events of the south Atlantic aside and, with Watford having made it into the top division for the first time in its history, I swore that I would attend every game, home and away.

It took some wheeling and dealing on the duties front but by the time the season schedule was published I was raring to go. And who wouldn't have been, faced with trips to some of the biggest clubs in the land?

As the season approached we began to hear rumblings on the terrace grapevine from supporters of other clubs, most of which were far from friendly. There were some especially nasty hooligan groups who made it quite clear that, as far as they were concerned, we were going to spend the season getting put firmly in our place. In short, we were going to get the shit kicked out of us at every opportunity.

On the pitch, things started astonishingly as the Watford team rampaged through the division and settled into life in the top half of the league table. We fans were also having a blast as we followed the team around the country and apart from the odd scuffle on away trips we encountered no real trouble.

That changed on November 27, 1982, when we traveled into north London and got our first serious taste of first division trouble against the team called Arsenal. To be honest, this game was the one I'd been most concerned about, primarily because they had sworn that they would have a go at us after the last time they played in our hometown. We arrived at the stadium just after 2 p.m. to find that the place was already packed. By about 2:45 it became apparent that a mob of Arsenal lads had sneaked in with us and were firmly ensconced at the back of the terrace. Worrying though this was, it was clear that the Watford lads were more than up for it.

Usually, I would have been among them but on this occasion I was, for some reason, standing about halfway down the terrace, leaning on a crush barrier with a meat pie in one hand and a cup of coffee in the other. I was still there when the first trouble kicked off and rapidly escalated into a major brawl. I can't say who started it but it quickly became clear that Watford was on top. Ferocious fighting was driving the Arsenal fans toward the exits.

Suddenly, as I watched on, a hand came out of nowhere and grabbed hold of my arm. I turned to find a middle-aged woman screaming at me to get up the back and help my mates. Totally shocked, I looked at her for a second and then simply handed her my cup, stuffed what was left of my pie in my mouth, and ducked under the barrier and headed up the terrace toward the battle that was still raging. But as soon as I stood up, a policeman appeared right in front of me and hit me full bore on the chin. In between the stars I was seeing I heard him shout at me, "Stay there, you cunt, I'll be back for you in a minute," and he vanished. But I couldn't move, even if I had wanted to. I simply fell back against the barrier and tried to remember where I was. By the time my head had cleared the trouble was over and the Arsenal lads had been banished. It was a victory for us, and although we expected them to have a go back at us after the game, we exited the stadium to find that they were nowhere to be seen. In fact, we didn't see any more trouble at all.

As the weeks passed, buoyed by our victory against Arsenal and with a team that was exceeding all expectations, we traveled the country full of confidence and made a nuisance of ourselves all over. At Liverpool, for example, some of their lads came into our end thinking they could take the piss and were battered senseless. However, things didn't always go our way, and we were occasionally on the receiving end of a few slaps. Nothing major but enough to warrant a few white lies when I went into work on a Monday morning.

The entire time I was "at it," no one at any of the military bases I was serving at had any idea of the things I was getting up to. I did everything I could to cover my tracks. That included tales of car crashes and muggings on the occasions where I had taken a beating. But it wasn't just that as a serviceman I could not afford to have the higher-ups find out. It was that I didn't *want* them to. What I did away from the base was mine and had nothing to do with them, although I doubt the military police would have considered it in quite the same way had I been caught.

As Christmas 1982 approached, fate threw another curve at me, this time in the shape of a woman. On every British military base, the cafés, bars, and shops are run by people who belong to an organization called the NAAFI (Navy, Army, and Air Force Institute), which is the U.S. equivalent of the commissary. On my base, we had mostly young women working for NAAFI, one of whom was called Tina. Thankfully, although she kept an eye on the results of her local hometown club, West Ham United, she had no real passion for soccer. But she understood that I did and was quite happy with my frequent trips to games the length and breadth of the country. In fact, the first time I took her to meet my parents, I strode in, introduced her to the family, and left her there while I went to watch Watford play Aston Villa.

As the season moved into 1983, our little mob of about

thirty or so lads had yet to come up against any serious op-position and, as such, we began to think that we were bet-ter than we were. We began to take risks. In February, we took one that was to have major, and painful, consequences. Especially for me. That, my friends, was the incident that opened this chapter. You remember, the one that involved a nail in my thigh. I told the people at work that my injuries were the result of a car accident, but when I told Tina the same thing she wasn't fooled.

Although she never actually said anything against what I was up to and certainly never tried to stop me from going to games, I realized that from that point on Tina was worried about me every time I headed for a game. As a consequence, I began to think seriously about what I was risking every time I pushed my luck. But with the team doing so well I just couldn't stop going, and in March we traveled to Coventry for what most people who were there regard as one of our finest hours.

I traveled on a bus. Not one of the official ones organized by the club, as these were strictly controlled and went direct-ly to the stadium, but on a bus that was arranged by one of the other lads. This was infinitely preferable because it meant that we could stop and have a drink on the way. For some reason, when we arrived at the stadium the police put us on a side terrace, well away from the rest of the Watford contingent and among a good number of local hooligan lads, none of whom were pleased to see us. As the game progressed, the locals began to creep over to us, and in the end we were surrounded by a group that not only looked decidedly nasty but also outnumbered us by about two to one. This quickly led to a couple of minor bouts of pushing and shoving as they tried to drive us out of "their" area, but we stood our ground and the police simply ushered the troublemakers away and stood watching while tensions mounted. When Watford scored what proved to be the winner, our celebrations were manic, which did their mood no good at all. But aside from a few more verbal exchanges not much else happened.

Once the game finished, the police took all the local lads away and kept us in the ground for about fifteen minutes. Instead of hanging around, we escaped around the back of the goal and down a steep set of stairs into the street. The second the last one of us was through the gates, the stewards slammed the gate behind us and we suddenly realized we were in the shit. There wasn't a policeman in sight and blocking our way were the lot who we had been winding up inside the ground, plus about fifty of their mates. We were outnumbered, and when they began to move toward us it was clear that unless we acted we were in for a major hammering. So we did the only thing we could: we went for it. My younger brother simply walked out into the road, saying,

"Come on then, you cunts! If you want it, let's go!" With that, as one we steamed across the road toward them.

To this day I don't know what they must have thought, but the second we started to run most of them bottled it and took off up the road while the rest were thrown over garden fences or simply slapped to the ground. We chased them for a while and then turned around to go back to the bus park. By then, however, they had regrouped and were blocking our way. With everyone on a major high, we steamed back in and ran them for a second time. By the time we got back to the bus park we were buzzing. When a few of them appeared on the other side of a fence and began throwing rocks from a railway line, we simply unleashed a volley of missiles at them and they vanished.

The journey home was something else. Although a few of us had picked up the odd bruise, most of us were unscathed, and the atmosphere on the coach was fantastic. It had been, as far as we were concerned, a major victory. After all, we had been away from home and outnumbered but had run their firm twice in a matter of minutes. For us, it didn't get any better than that.

For the next few weeks we became an even bigger pain in the backside than we had been and played up whenever the opportunity arose. With the team doing so well it was hard not to get caught up in the euphoria, and I became increasingly wrapped up in what was happening on the pitch as opposed to off it, namely Tina.

However, as April approached and I fell even deeper for her, things other than my worries about her began to influence my behavior on match days, not least of which was that the military handed me the opportunity to convert to permanent flying duties. For most males this is a dream job and I was no exception. Aware that getting arrested would have a major and very damaging impact on my service record, I began to step back from trouble altogether. I had never been the first one in but now I was usually among the last. That's if I made it to the games at all. It was becoming increasingly clear that word of our activities was spreading through the hooligan grapevine, with the result that clubs were making stronger efforts to teach us a lesson. By the time the biggest game of the season approached, I had made the decision that once the season was over I would give up away travel and simply go to home games as a fan.

Up to that point, traveling around following Watford had always been a huge laugh. While the threat of violence had been an ever-present part of the experience, as it was for just about every soccer fan back then, it wasn't the primary reason why we traveled around as a group. That had pretty much always been watching the Golden Boys and having fun. Not to say we bottled it whenever anyone tried to have a go—far from it. Whenever we were together if someone wanted a row with us then we'd give them one. Sometimes we'd come out on top; other times, if we were seriously out-numbered, we'd do a runner, and a few times we even took a kicking. It was the way it was, we accepted that, and it all added to the excitement. Although there were certain games where we knew instinctively that trouble was going to happen, the one thing we never really did was go to a game looking to start trouble ourselves. That was to change on April 4, 1983, when for the first and only time I went to a game with the sole intention of getting stuck into someone.

Now I'm sure a shrink would say that the reason for this was because I had a deep-rooted need to prove myself to my peers or that I had post-Falkland issues I needed to get out of my system. To be honest, although I suspect there is some mileage in that, there is a more fundamental reason. You see the team we were playing was one I had already grown to detest. Our local, and very bitter, rivals Luton Town. To be honest, "rivals" isn't the right word. It's way too soft. This was, and is, hatred. Pure and simple.

Now Watford's home end had traditionally been the Rookery, but for various reasons we had been moved to the other end of the ground known as the Red Lion end, on account of the Red Lion bar just across the road. It was a sprawling, uncovered terrace that held upwards of 7,000 people, and even before kickoff, trouble had broken out in the town. Meanwhile, inside the stadium, we'd been scuffling with Luton fans who had been stupid enough to try and infiltrate our terrace.

By early '83 many hooligan groups around the country had given themselves names such as the Inter City Firm (West Ham) and the Zulu Army (Birmingham City). At Watford no such thing existed. Watford consisted of small groups from towns near the ground, and although we all knew each other it was rare that we actually stood together. Indeed, it is reasonable to say that some of the groups didn't even get on. However, this game was something different, and once it had finished, as news broke that the police would be holding the Luton fans back for a while to ease the threat of violence outside, word went around the entire end that we were going for it and everyone was to hang back, mob up, and then go after Luton's firm. Within five minutes there were about 150 lads there, all wound up and ready. Suddenly a shout went up, and before I knew it I was in the middle of this pack running toward the junction where the Luton support would emerge. As soon as we saw them all hell broke lose. Initially, they ran and ended up in St. Mary's Road, where they stopped and confronted us. We surged forward and, grabbing anything we could out of the front gardens on either side, unleashed a hail of missiles at them. Eventually, the police arrived and drove us apart, forcing the Luton fans down the road. But we weren't finished yet. We ran the short distance along Merton Road to Market Street, our plan being to hit them again in the center of town. But as we got halfway down Market Street, the police appeared in front of us and formed a line right across the road. Clearly, there was no way through. We turned to go back, only to find that the police had got in behind us as well. We were now effectively sealed in Market Street. They kept us there for what seemed an age, releasing us only when the Luton hooligans had been forced on trains out of town and our adrenaline had run down.

As we walked slowly back to my car, I realized then exactly what I was risking and decided enough was enough. Although I continued to go to every game until the end of that season, and carried on for a good deal of the next, my days as a so-called hooligan were all but over. There were still the odd times when it was unavoidable, but they were rare and, if I could, I talked my way out of trouble rather than fight.

By the time I left the forces in 1994, trouble at games was widely believed to be a thing of the past. The death of ninety-six Liverpool fans at Hillsborough in 1989 had been the apparent catalyst for the change. Now we had a whole new type of soccer, all seater stadia and corporate money. Motorway rest stops positively welcomed soccer fans instead of barring them, and the High Streets of England were no longer the war zones they had been in the mid-eighties. The hooligan was, as far as most people were concerned, history. This was, as any soccer fan of the time will tell you, total bullshit. I still went to games when I could and all too often ran a gauntlet of hate. But where once I enjoyed the atmosphere that accompanies confrontation and the apprehension that goes with away travel, now I'd become sick of it. I saw the police becoming not far short of an unarmed army and I began to believe that soccer could be better than this.

I wasn't alone either. By the late 1980s all of the lads I'd watched games with for ten years had left the violence behind, as had almost every soccer fan I knew. Some due to age, others due to wives and families, most, like me, due to boredom. But deep inside we are still those same lads and as I said earlier, when we get the chance to spend time together and reminisce, we look back on those times as some of the best of our lives. Fun? Fuck me, you don't know the half of it.

CHAPTER TWO

Rivalry

Cut me and I'll bleed yellow!

Since you're reading this I'm guessing you're a bit of a sports fan. You follow baseball maybe? Okay, let me make a suggestion to you. I want you and a group of your friends to watch every single baseball game your local team plays. Not on the television but live in the stadium. Not just the home ones either; I want you to travel all over the U.S. and follow your team when they're on the road. As you're watching the games, I want you to sing and shout your support for your guys but I also want you to be abusive toward the opposing team. Just as important, I want you to be abusive toward the opposing fans, some of whom will abuse you right back. Occasionally, this will result in tempers flaring, and once in a while you'll end up fighting, not only with groups of like-minded people who follow other teams but with the police who will do their utmost to keep you apart from each other.

Over the years— yes, years— these fights will develop into an intense rivalry, and you will learn not simply to dislike opposing fans but to hate them with a burning passion. This passion will last a lifetime and be taken up by your kids, and their kids.

On top of that, to paraphrase Tyler Durden in the movie *Fight Club*, you must adopt the mantra, "You do not talk about anything to do with this with anyone who isn't involved." That means everyone from family and workmates to the police. No one will ever know. It will become, in effect, your secret life. One that will consume you for the rest of your days but that will allow you to prove yourself as a man and also give you both the worst and the very best of times. It's also something that could, if it all goes horribly wrong, cost you either your liberty or even your life.

Fancy that? Of course not. You're a sports fan, not a fighter. Fighting's something idiots do in bars. You'd be bloody crazy even to think about it, wouldn't you? Yet plenty do, and have. I did. And all in the name of soccer. A sport that many die-hard American sports fans regard as little more than a joke.

So what it is about soccer that invokes such emotions in people that they will willingly indulge in intimidation, violence, and even murder in its name? Just as important, why not any other sport? Because if what most people are led to believe is correct, hooliganism is unique to soccer. Other sports are usually watched in an atmosphere of tranquility, devoid of any aggression at all. This, of course, is total bullshit. Almost every mainstream sport has experienced crowd violence of sorts, be it rugby, basketball, boxing, ice hockey, or motor sports.

There is, however, a marked distinction between crowd violence and sports violence. If players or officials become involved in anything serious then, no matter what the sporting discipline, it quite rightly becomes news. Big news! When the French soccer player Zinedine Zidane landed a headbutt on the Italian defender Marco Materazzi during the 2006 World Cup final, the impact was felt around the globe. And I defy any sports fan to hear the name Mike Tyson and not think of what he did to Evander Holyfield.

In part, it is the sheer rarity of such incidents that makes them so sensational, but the same cannot be said outside of the sporting arena. Even the traditionally serene sport of cricket has witnessed some serious problems with crowd trouble in recent years, primarily at the international level but also at English county level. Admittedly such cases are usually different in nature to the kind of thing seen at soccer. But they are problems nevertheless, and we should not hide the fact that they take place, even though the governing bodies of many of these sports are happy if we do so. In addition, the media have become so apathetic toward the issue of crowd violence that unless something happens to mark it out as sensational, they don't even bother reporting it. And when they do, if it isn't soccer-related, they rarely, if ever, call it hooliganism, even though that is exactly what it is.

Undeniably, soccer does attract a sizable minority of normally rational people who do not simply shake hands after a good game and have a beer and a laugh together, but instead step over that line and take things further by becoming a part of something that is really a sinister subculture akin to gang warfare. The academics have their theories about social depravation and rebellion to explain why this is, but to me, even if I placed any credence in them, which I don't, these are excuses, not causes. In my opinion, the vast majority of hooliganism as we know it today is caused by one of three factors: passion, reputation, and, most important, history.

In the United States, soccer might languish behind other mainstream sports such as baseball, football, basketball, and even NASCAR, but it is undeniably the most popular game on the planet. It is played from dawn till dusk by kids the world over, and as supporters we are force-fed it via TV, newspapers, or obsessed parents. Millions of us even spend a good portion of our income going to watch it. As fans, our links with our chosen clubs become a part of our personality to such an extent that many soccer fans, myself included, regard themselves as an integral and essential element of the team and the team as an essential part of them. We use expressions such as "Cut me and I'll bleed yellow" (yellow, of course, is Watford's team color) or "I'm a Gooner" in the same way we'd say "I'm an engineer" and expect people to know just what that means. Our clubs are followed through thick and thin, and we accept the bad times in the hope that one day the good ones will come along so that we can enjoy them as well. In short, we support their efforts on our behalf. As fans, it is what we do. But that support is far more than simply financial. Yes, we hand over our ticket money, but we also bring with us something that money cannot buy: passion.

I make no bones about this and I'm certainly not ashamed to say it—I love Watford. She is my mistress. She's given me some of the most joyous moments of my life as well as some of the worst. I've wept buckets for her and fought for her and will continue to cherish our relationship until the day I die. I have even passed that love on to my own son who is now 100 percent Golden Boy and as passionate about Watford as I ever was. Passion is what breathes life into any club, be it for a small amateur team or one watched by a crowd of 80,000. Indeed, many supporters believe, with some justification, that they are the heart and soul of their club. After all, the players and the staff are simply passing through and will be gone one day, but fans will carry the aspirations of their club with them until their dying day. That may sound dramatic if you're not a soccer fan, but believe me it is uncannily accurate. We want our clubs to be the best of the best. More important, when it happens, we want to claim our part and be able to say we did our bit. That's why soccer fans resent those who jump on bandwagons, be they our own or even others.

Anyone can suddenly come out and say they support Liverpool or Manchester United but they are not true supporters. Not really. They are simply glory hunters who are hijacking the loyalty shown by others and riding along on the back of current success. Don't get me wrong, I've often whiled away a boring 0–0 draw against clubs like Bury or Rotherham wondering why I support Watford and didn't stick it out at Chelsea, cursing myself for inflicting a lifetime of misery on my poor son. But I know that you can't just change clubs because times are bad. Do that, and you have no right to enjoy the good times or, for that matter, to call yourself a fan. Being a soccer supporter isn't just about watching great soccer; it's about putting time in and belonging to something, the entity that is a soccer club.

As a brief glance at any newspaper will show you, this

level of passion inevitably manifests itself as some kind of rivalry, something never more true than among soccer fans. We all want our clubs to be the best, but to do that it stands to reason that they have to defeat other teams. Soccer is, after all, a competitive sport. So when our team plays, we sing, chant, and shout to spur them on in the hope that they will react to us and do the business on our behalf. This fervor is never more important than when a team faces a local rival.

For all soccer fans, local derby games are the single most important games of the year because they involve that most significant of factors, bragging rights. If I had a dollar for every time I've heard the phrase "I don't care how we do this season, as long as we beat those wankers," I would be a wealthy man indeed.

I have been to matches that have been played in atmospheres so hostile, I half-expected the United Nations to turn up. Make no mistake—rivalries between fans of local clubs often extend way beyond match days. Often they impact everyday life.

I am as guilty of this kind of behavior as anyone. My lifelong hatred of Luton Town bears on just about everything I do or have done in my life. From an early age, I banned the color orange—the primary color of their team strip—from my house, and both of my daughters were told that if they ever dared to bring a Luton fan home, he could wait outside while

I packed their bags. My son, being a Watford fan, would obviously never entertain a girl from Luton anyway.

Furthermore, all tradesmen who come to my front door are quizzed about their supporting allegiances—Luton fans being sent packing, obviously—and I will never, ever drive a General Motors car because that corporation is the main employer in Luton. To be fair, because I am a fairly high profile Watford fan, they feel the same about me and sales of my books in Luton's bookstores barely register. Fine by me. I wouldn't want their dirty money anyway.

It doesn't stop there. Back in the old days, I had a 1960s-era Ford. Big bastard thing it was, similar to the old Crown Victoria, and it was my pride and joy. I had all kinds of plans to stick a Chevy V8 in it, but because it could carry six people in great comfort it was instead adopted as our away-day transport and we went bloody everywhere in it. I think we went to something like twenty away games by car that year and we had a fantastic time. It just seemed that every trip we went on was an adventure of some kind. From blocking rush-hour traffic into Southampton when we broke down to one of us almost crashing through the roof of a gas station when he tried to retrieve our football, there was never a dull moment. But the highlight was one of those things that you simply never forget and never tire of talking about because it was bloody hilarious.

We were on our way to see Watford play at Nott's County and for once there were only five people in the old girl so there was even more room than usual. As we were turning onto the freeway, we looked to see if there were any Watford lads hitching, but what did we see but a Luton fan with a scarf on and his thumb out. We could not believe our luck. It was a dream come true!

So we pulled over and he came running up. "Are you going to Luton, lads?" he asked.

"Of course," we cried. "Jump in and we'll drop you at the Arndale," which is the shopping mall near their shithole of a stadium.

The poor bastard was so happy and was chattering away like a good 'un about how he was looking forward to the game and what result he hoped for. How we kept from laughing I'll never know. I think he must have first realized something was wrong when we drove past the Luton turnoff in the outside lane doing about seventy miles per hour and he fell gradually more silent the farther north we headed. Finally, he piped up although I suspect he already knew the answer. "You *are* going to Luton, aren't you?"

The answer was simple. "We go to Shit Town once a year, mate, when Watford play there, and today you're coming with us to see the Hornets play, so just sit still, be quiet, and don't you dare fucking move."

His face was a bloody picture. Not only was he not going to see his team, but he was being taken miles away by people who supported the local opposition and there was nothing at all he could do about it. From then on we just ignored him and carried on talking as usual. The poor bastard had to spend an hour or so listening to how much we hated his team, their ground, and their shit fans.

When we arrived on the outskirts of Nottingham, about ninety miles north of where he wanted to be, we stopped the car and told him to get out but to leave his scarf as a memento. "You mean you're not going to take me back to Hemel?" The stupidity of that question has made me smile for years. It certainly made all of us roar with laughter as we drove off leaving him by the side of the road.

I have no idea how he got home—I don't really care—but he gave us the greatest laugh I have ever had at soccer. The look on his face as I watched him in my rearview mirror was absolutely classic.

So important are these rivalries that whenever a group of soccer lads gather, sooner or later talk is going to turn to how much you hate the rival fans and what you'd do to get one over on them if you got the chance. We Watford fans are no different. The thing is, as we've gotten older, this antagonism to the rival team's fans has actually moved on into real life. For example, I have a mate who is a solicitor and he has always refused point-blank to represent any Luton fan because, in his words, "I'd rather the cunt lost the case and went down."

Another of my mates used to be a fireman, and one night his company got a call to a house on fire. The family escaped the house unharmed, but my mate and his comrades still had to put out the blaze. My mate was assigned to go in with the breathing apparatus on and went through the front door with his hose on. After dealing with the fire contained on the ground floor, he began to go through all upstairs rooms to check to see that it hadn't progressed. After he pushed this one door open what did he see? Luton Town posters on the wall! The bed even had a Luton Town quilt on it!

Well, naturally, my mate was outraged, so of course he put the hose on full power and blasted the shit out of this bedroom. Within seconds the room and everything in it was absolutely fucked. His boss went mental at him but what could he do? The place had been on fire, after all. The kid whose bedroom it was freaked out, and his mood wasn't helped when my mate told him to get a life and watch a decent club. He had a point as far as I was concerned.

The worst tale of local rivalry I ever heard involves something so gross even I would think twice about its legitimacy, even in the name of the club. And I most certainly wouldn't want it done to me. The story was told to me a few years back by a fellow ex-serviceman I met on holiday. In case you don't know, the rivalry between the two Glasgow clubs extends way beyond soccer. Celtic has its roots in the Catholic community while Rangers are strictly Protestant, and as we saw for decades in Northern Ireland the two don't usually see eye to eye.

Anyway, a Celtic fan was at the end of a week of guard duty during which time his sergeant, a staunch Rangers fan, had been winding him up about how shit Celtic were and putting him on all the worst shifts possible. Since he was two ranks down the chain of command, there had been nothing he could do without risking any kind of disciplinary backlash, and so he had been forced to simply take it. However, by the last night, he'd sworn to himself that he would exact revenge. When the sergeant arrived for the night shift with a dish full of pasta for his evening meal, our man knew exactly what he would do.

The first chance he got, he took the bowl out of the refrigerator and jerked off into it. He then stirred the whole thing up, put it back on the shelf, and sat back to wait. Later that night, totally oblivious to the seasoning that had been added to his evening meal, the sergeant devoured the lot much to the amusement of the Celtic fan, who simply sat back and watched.

The following morning, as the Celtic fan made ready to

leave the guardroom for the last time, he took the sergeant to one side and, after asking him if he'd enjoyed his pasta, told him exactly what he'd done. I'll leave you to imagine how quickly the contents of the guy's stomach reappeared.

Stories as extreme as this are, thankfully, reasonably rare, which is something of a relief if only for reasons of taste. However, the fact remains that the fierce passion behind these rivalries is an integral and welcome part of the supporting experience. I certainly derive a great deal of pleasure from hating Luton and everything associated with it, not least because it gives me something else to do when I'm not at games. But it is very much a personal thing. At games, things are different.

I might curse under my breath if I see someone wearing a Luton shirt in my hometown but I wouldn't stand there and hurl abuse at him. I'd sure as shit do it if I was within a mile of Vicarage Road on the day we were playing them because then I would be free of the normal restrictions placed on me by society. That freedom is one of the main reasons people go to soccer games; the banter between fans is not only a vital ingredient of the match day atmosphere, it's one of the most enjoyable.

Think about it, you're in your section of the stadium cheering on your team and abusing the visitors while at the other end of the ground is a group of rival fans who also aspire to victory. Generally, no matter what the nature of the banter, the atmosphere created is good-natured, but on occasion it can switch and spill over into hostility or worse. Something might happen on the pitch, be it a bad foul or a controversial decision, and the mood will suddenly go from jovial to aggressive. Usually, that aggression will evaporate as soon as the final whistle goes or, if it doesn't, it will show only in bad moods or moaning. And as you walk away from the stadium, the smiles will return and by the time you're in the pub or the car it will almost be forgotten. After all, you cannot change something that has already become a part of history.

The problems come when that aggression is not forgotten but is instead carried along. Sometimes, it will even spill over into something else. Generally speaking, this is the essential difference between "normal" fans and hooligans. For the latter, and I now include myself in that group, taking those rivalries and passions out of the ground and beyond what most people would regard as acceptable is not only routine, it is an essential part of their match day experience. For them, what happens off the pitch is as equally important as what happens on it because they regard the reputation of the team and the fans as one and the same. If someone does something to affect that result, be it a player or a rival mob, they will try and redress the balance by extracting revenge in the only way they can. It is the fact that they overstep that boundary that marks them out as hooligans and what they do as hooliganism.

You need only think of a certain club in Southeast London to understand how far hooligans will go when it comes to defending their reputation. If ever a club evoked instant thoughts of crowd violence, it is Millwall. Even today, twenty-odd years later, the memory of one of the most famous riots in English soccer's shameful history is as vivid as it was when the television news broadcast it to a shocked nation.

The background to the incident is simple. In March 1985, the Millwall fans traveled to Kenilworth Road for an FA Cup quarter-final tie against Luton. The club took thousands of supporters to the game including a large number of hooligans. So many supporters arrived that the police, already on full alert, rounded up the fans and forced them into the ground as quickly as they could. However, the enclosure for the visiting supporters was far too small and the place was soon absolutely crammed. The problems began almost immediately.

Minutes after the game started they spilled out onto the pitch, delaying the game for twenty-five minutes. Once the match restarted, a number of fights broke out in various parts of the ground but these were quickly dealt with by an increasingly nervous police force. With Millwall losing 1–0 and only ten minutes to go, several hundred fans spilled onto the touchline in an attempt to force the abandonment of the game. They pushed their way through the police cordon onto the pitch but were repelled twice before the referee, himself a police inspector and determined to finish the game, blew for full-time. As soon as the whistle sounded, the Millwall fans flooded onto the pitch and immediately headed for the seated enclosure where they ripped out seats and attacked the police with them. The police then regrouped and baton-charged the Millwall fans, who first pulled back and then attacked again. Other Millwall fans poured onto the pitch and astonishing scenes took place as the police, stewards, and Millwall fans fought for control of the pitch. Eventually the Millwall fans began to calm down, but as they were driven out of the ground they kicked things off again, causing untold damage to houses and cars outside the stadium and wrecking the train taking them back to London. It was an episode that left forty-seven people, including thirty-one policemen, injured.

What made matters even worse was the fact that the violence had been screened on television and the entire country had watched open-mouthed as the events unfolded before their very eyes. So bad were they in fact that they continue to be shown with monotonous regularity. As a result, the events of that day formed, or rather enhanced, a reputation that has stuck with Millwall ever since despite the best efforts of the club to remove it. But the fact that such a reputation exists has two key consequences. The first is that many people outside the game, and a few within it, continue to think that hooliganism and Millwall are inseparable, which means that all Millwall fans, old or new, are immediately tainted. The second is that when the Millwall club—and the same applies to any club with a history of trouble—travels around the county, the police will be on the offensive and the locals will be either hiding or looking to confront them to build up their own reputation and, as a result, their own history. Such an attitude does no favors for the decent, law-abiding members of the clubs who only want to watch a game of soccer and not be herded around like sheep or abused by rival fans whenever they travel away.

Conversely, if you take my own club, Watford, which has long been known as the "family club," the idea of it being associated with any degree of soccer violence astonishes some people. When they come to Vicarage Road, visiting supporters do not expect to experience trouble nor do they when the Watford fans visit their stadium, and in the main they do not. Yet despite this image the club has always had a small element of troublemakers among its support, of which I was once a part. In recent times, a new group has surfaced at Watford and eventually, by traveling around and fronting up more active hooligan firms, their reputation will grow to the extent that when they play Watford, other firms will expect

47

trouble and so will bring trouble when they come. Something that will have an impact on everyone else at the club.

Yet while most people will concede that reputations cause problems in and of themselves, we should not forget that if a group of fans has become saddled with a reputation, it will be richly deserved. Reputations, like respect, are earned. Furthermore, there will be people who play up to those reputations and so, in effect, keep them going. And while certain groups may go through periods of inactivity, every so often they will explode back onto the scene and let everyone know they are still active.

Rivalries of course do not have to be localized. They can start in all kinds of ways. For example, if a club or even a city experiences some kind of tragedy it is sadly inevitable that at some point a group of rival fans will use it to upset or taunt their opposite numbers. Manchester United have suffered more than most from this as songs about the 1958 Munich air crash— where many of the top players on the clubs roster were killed—have been heard at many grounds over the years. Similarly, back in the eighties Leeds United supporters were taunted with songs claiming that the Yorkshire Ripper—a notorious serial killer of the time—was beating the local prostitutes 12–0. Furthermore, for years Tottenham fans were subjected to groups of rival fans hissing at them for many seasons due to their supposed links with the Jewish community. The hissing was supposed to replicate the noise of the gas chambers of Auschwitz. Thankfully, that is one particular taunt that seems to have disappeared, but the notion of using tragedy to cause offense lingers on.

One of the clearest examples of this taunting based on history involves two clubs who are party to one of the most long-standing and violent rivalries in English soccer. They are the two Welsh clubs, Cardiff City and Swansea City.

The history of confrontation involving these fans is long and bloody. Yet despite the many thousands of incidents between the two sets of supporters over the years, there is one that causes more controversy than any of the others because both sides regard it with different levels of importance. It is known in hooligan circles as "the swim-away story."

If you talk to followers of the two clubs, you will hear hundreds of different versions of this incident. Indeed, it now seems that there were actually two episodes. The first took place on a May bank holiday in the early 1970s, when some Swansea fans were attacked by a group of Cardiff supporters in a Welsh holiday resort called Barry Island. But the second, and most important, took place in Swansea toward the end of the '80s.

The basic facts as I have uncovered them are these. Cardiff had traveled to Swansea and, as usual, was busy causing mayhem in the city center. The Cardiff group, the PVM

(Pure Violence Mob) from Port Talbot, was playing an active part in this but, for some reason, about ten of them had traveled independently of the main party and rather than go into the city center had made their way down to the seafront. Unfortunately, they ran into a large Swansea mob and came under attack. Despite standing for a time, the PVM lads were forced to run into the sea to escape the Swansea fans and ended up standing chest deep in the water. Rather than follow them in, the locals began bombarding them with rocks until the police came and rescued them.

Despite the Cardiff fans' assertions that this was only a minor defeat and had more to do with the numbers involved than the quality of their firm, the incident quickly settled into local folklore and even now, more than ten years later, Swansea fans will taunt their Cardiff opponents by mimicking the front crawl. It usually has the desired effect and, as a result, it is unlikely it will ever be forgotten.

The one constant in all of the events above is history. Soccer fans have long memories and hooligans even longer ones, and if something has happened in the past to fire up anger or rivalry between two sets of fans, inevitably, one day someone will do something to exact revenge or exploit it. It could be as simple as walking around a corner and getting a slap from an irate Norwich fan or as frightening as entering a tube station teeming with West Ham. And if you are part of a mob and someone gives you a beating or gains any kind of result against you, you are duty-bound to respond and gain revenge. This is why I firmly believe that history is the most important factor behind trouble at soccer. The tragedy is that you simply cannot change what has already happened, yet to a large extent hooliganism is all about the desire to do just that.

CHAPTER THREE

The Firms

Arrogance is the key.

To outsiders, a group of soccer lads might look, sound, and act like they've all come from the same mold, but to those in the know it is clear who is a real hooligan and who isn't. You see, it isn't simply what you wear or do; it's the way you wear it and do it. Arrogance is the key, and you get that only with time and experience.

To some, a hooligan is someone as simple and innocent as a teenage kid in a replica jersey walking along singing. But to others a hooligan is someone who starts an attack on rival fans by hurling a brick through the plate-glass window of a packed bar or by spraying mace into a train-carriage full of people. The reason for these diverging views is that an individual's perception of what constitutes a hooligan can be decided in only one of two ways: either by their own experiences or via the media. There is no other way.

For those who have actually tasted the rough end of soccer hooligans, be they fans of the game themselves or not, their perception of both hooliganism and hooligans will be all too real. Anyone who has ever been confronted with a baying mob knows how frightening it can be, but if you have no experience of it, it can be absolutely terrifying. The simple truth is that "hooliganism" is a blanket term that can be applied to any kind of antisocial behavior that damages the image of soccer, whether it's foul and abusive chanting or fifty lads ambushing a bar using baseball bats. As a descriptive word, "hooliganism" is valuable only to the media, the police, and irate politicians, but as a culture of group violence it is bloody fascinating.

"Group" is the key word here. As I have already mentioned, hooliganism is very much a gang activity. In that respect it has a number of similarities to gang culture in the United States. For example, both gangs and hooligans are built on the notion of trust, family, and loyalty and exist not only to protect reputations and turf, but also to provide safety in numbers.

Similarly, most have a structure that develops over time with a central core of seasoned fighters, led by Top Boys, who rise through the ranks by being either the most violent or the best organizers. Make no mistake, these Top Boys have power. At some of the bigger so-called superfirms, they can call on between four hundred and five hundred fighters. That's a bloody army!

A great example of this structure was provided by Millwall hooligans in a BBC documentary first shown in 1977. Far from being nothing more than a messy collection of thugs, the hooligans at Millwall had a clearly defined hierarchy. To begin with, for kids aged fourteen and under, they belonged to the Half-Way Liners and their role was to find out where the opposing fans were before games and then wind them up during matches.

These kids would then graduate to become members of the Treatment, known for their abusive and aggressive chanting, and then, if they proved themselves worthy, went on to the most feared group of all, F-Troop. Named after a popular TV program of the time, they were legendary for being fearless and very violent fighters.

A key difference between hooligan groups and many of the gangs that exist in American cities is motivation. Generally speaking, hooligans are not motivated by anything other than a love of soccer and though there are always exceptions, as a collective they rarely become involved in non-soccer related violence. Indeed, membership in a hooligan group is very much a part-time activity in that it only really becomes relevant on the day of a match. This allows firm members to forge a kind of secret life that only they and the other members of the group know about, giving them the freedom to behave in a manner that is more often than not totally at odds with the way they behave in the comfort of their own homes or at their place of work.

I, for example, used all kinds of deviousness to hide my match day activities from everyone I worked with. I never even discussed it with lads who I know full well had been involved with mobs at their own clubs before they enlisted. This anonymity added to the excitement for me because it was another layer of "getting away with it."

There is, of course, much more to being a part of a hooligan firm than simply running around with a gang. Much more. There is a certain code of honor among the hooligan firms, one that draws specific boundaries marking what is and is not acceptable behavior. For example, if you and your lads receive a battering at the hands of a rival mob, you do not go the police and complain about it, you simply get your revenge next time around. That's the way it works.

If you take my own tale about getting beaten up in Swansea as an example, this phenomenon becomes clear. The Saturday following my kicking at Swansea, Watford had no game and so we mobbed up and headed for Tottenham where Swansea was the visiting team. Our aim was to exact some kind of revenge for what had happened to me. If their hooligan firm was in London that day, however, we never found them, and in the end we had to leave the Tottenham ground early as some of the local hooligans were becoming decidedly unhappy with our presence.

Among many old-school hooligans the use of knives is wholly unacceptable, and I've heard many a tale of younger lads receiving serious beatings for pulling a blade out and waving it around. Quite rightly, too!

For many of the individuals involved in those most bizarre of cultures, the fact that these boundaries are in place seems to reinforce subconsciously the belief that hooliganism is nothing more than a game.

In a sense, there is actually a genuine feeling in the hooligan community that while the police might treat soccer violence as one of the most serious of crimes—something reflected in the amount of time they pour into fighting it and the severity of the sentences handed out for it— it isn't really a proper crime. After all, if a group of lads want to fight with another group of lads who in return want to fight with them, what's the problem? It's not like the old days when towns were shut down on match days for fear of hooliganism and fans had to be fenced in to keep groups apart.

A simple analogy can be made with avoiding taxes. Most of us have either done it at one time or know someone who has, and we all know that it's against the law. Yet if we hear of someone who has done it do we report them as we really should? No, we don't. Because tax avoidance isn't regarded as a proper crime, and if the bloke gets caught, we think of him as being unlucky.

Hooliganism is exactly the same because even when people know who the participants are, as most people do at most clubs, do they ever grass them to the authorities? Of course not. Instead the offenders are simply thought of as being a bit of a rogue and so there is no stigma attached.

Yet if you look at the bigger picture, this apathy, from both other soccer fans and the game itself, is allowing the people involved to continue their activities pretty much un-molested. As a result, they are able to justify to themselves their behavior because no one else seems to care. And for some people it is the getting away with it all that is the main attraction. Only when they end up in court and the anonym-ity they have enjoyed is removed does the full realization and consequences of what they have been doing, as well as risking, hit home. That's when they are stigmatized and more often than not, ostracized.

Another reason people become involved in hooligan groups is more of a recent phenomenon. It's one that has sparked a great deal of debate and there are plenty who say the very idea is bullshit. I myself was firmly in that camp of dissenters for a long time. But a while back I got into a conversation with a group of lads at Watford. As we talked about clothes, books, and the movie *Green Street Hooligans*, there was a particular thing about them that struck me. The majority were from single-parent families.

The more I reflected on it, the more it interested me, and so I began to do a bit of digging around, not just at my own club but at others as well. As I did so, I began to suspect that the demise of the traditional family has had quite a profound impact on the hooligan scene.

While the terraces have long provided the perfect environment for males to indulge in the kind of same-sex bonding that is vital to our gender's limited emotional growth, the sense of "second family" that derives from such camaraderie also has the potential to provide something else. While it might not have been relevant to either me or the lads I knew when I was in my teens, it is clearly vital to many of the youngsters I've spoken to in recent years. Few of them have ever previously experienced such a feeling and were maybe even unaware of how important it was until they came to walk through a turnstile. I am talking about a compelling and powerful male influence.

It is undoubtedly a sad reflection of modern-day Britain that there are so many teenage lads who have little or no father figure at home and sadder still to think that, for some, the only opportunity they have to mix socially with older males comes via the Saturday scene. But for many young- sters that is the reality. The worry is that this influence al- most certainly will a negative one.

Thankfully, there will be plenty of lads for whom a sense of right and wrong will be strong enough to limit any antisocial behavior to little more than a swagger and a bit of cockiness, but there are others who become involved in hooliganism for whom this will clearly not apply. For them, involvement with a group of lads provides not only a much-needed sense of be- longing but also, in many respects, a sense of purpose. And among their number are plenty who crave the kind of respect that peer recognition provides. These lads in particular are a real danger. For they seem to have little or no intention of wait- ing for their acceptance into the ranks but instead readily put themselves into situations where they are all but demanding attention. When you consider few have little or no respect for law and order anyway, then you can see why at certain clubs we have youths with an almost feral sense of passion for the firm they aspire to be a central part of. After all, it provides them with things that they cannot get elsewhere and that rapidly become incredibly important to them as individuals.

The fact that the entire scene is governed by a set of unwritten rules and boundaries lends the whole thing a kind of "honor among thieves" legitimacy that allows the participants to justify to themselves why they behave in the way that they do. It also explains why increasing numbers not only consider a banning order as akin to a badge of honor but also actually regard prison as an occupational hazard.

The reality is that very few of the people involved in hooliganism will ever end up in court. They will simply carry on until they drift out of direct involvement in the cycle of weekly violence because of age or boredom. That is, after all, what happened to me. I grew up and realized that the whole thing was extremely dangerous, and also bloody stupid!

That's not to say they everyone who draws back from hooliganism will give it up entirely, because a good portion of them won't. They will still turn out for big games such as local derbies and will always think of themselves as a part of their particular firm. Some of them may become legends themselves. Indeed, among the hooligan fraternity are legions of names that are as much a part of English soccer's history as Sir Stanley Mathews or David Beckham, and they are held in very high regard by their peers.

Some, such as Bill Gardner, widely regarded as the central figure in the formation of West Ham United's ICF (Inter City Firm), have even gone on to write about their activities with great success. Indeed, in recent years the publishing world has witnessed an explosion of what has become known as hoolie lit, which, if anything, has lent the Saturday scene an additional legitimacy, reinforced by the fact that even Hollywood has tackled the subject with the movie *Green Street Hooligans*. The result is that new people are drawn in and the circle of violence continues unbroken.

The irony is of course that as the guy who wrote the screenplay for *Green Street Hooligans,* as well as twelve books covering different aspects of the issue of soccer violence, I have to take my share of the blame. Now who would have ever thought that was going to happen? Not me, that's for sure. I'm bloody glad it has, though.

Many people who follow the culture of soccer will have heard of West Ham United's ICF and the Chelsea Headhunters but groups such as Barnsley's Five-0, the Cardiff Soul Crew, or Stoke City's Naughty 40 are every bit as dangerous and, to the hooligans themselves, every bit as famous. And so over the past few years, I have tried to piece together what I believe is the definitive listing of these firms. As you can appreciate, this has been a time-consuming process and I have relied on many people for help and information. The difficulty with something like this, of course, is separating fact from fiction. Some of the names on this list are so ridiculous; I still wonder if they are the figment of someone's overactive imagination. Therefore, I have included only a tiny selection, and these are names that I have been able to confirm or that I was already aware of.

Before I carry on, I must stress that not all these groups still exist. Some of the names on this list were consigned to history long ago although it is fairly reasonable to assume that many of them will simply have adopted new tags even though they have pretty much the same membership. Indeed, this is a fairly routine tactic to either throw off the attentions of the police or reemerge after a particularly serious and humiliating beating. Others on the list will simply have been swallowed up and incorporated into other firms, while a few—but not many—will have been smashed by the activities of the police. What is more, it is almost certain that others will have been formed since this book went to press. For in spite of the oppressive policing in England, new groups seem to be springing up all the time.

It is also important to understand that some clubs do have more than one active firm attached to them, although this was much more prevalent in the early eighties than it is today, while some clubs simply do not have any kind of "named" firm attached to them at all. But that does not mean such clubs do not have a violent element. Far from it. What it might mean is that they are either inactive or simply fragmented.

My own club, Watford, provides a good example of this, for although in my day we had no real firm as such, what we did have were a number of little groups of lads, all of whom were game. But although we all knew one another by sight, we rarely, if ever, traveled together let alone fought together. Sometimes, we even fought *with* each other! I have no idea why this was. Indeed, I sometimes wonder what it would have been like had we all banded together and actually formed a proper firm. We certainly proved on more than a few occasions that we would have had the numbers. Even today there are some serious-looking lads to be found on the terraces at Vicarage Road. Hence the fairly recent formation of groups such as the Watford Youth Aggro (WYA).

Another thing to note is that not every member of a firm is a hooligan. Indeed, if you look at a club such as Birmingham City, a good proportion of the support think of themselves as a part of the entity that is called the Zulu Army because it is a label that the fans have happily attached to themselves. Yet while within that group is a large and very active group of hooligans who also call themselves the Zulu Army, the bulk of the Blues support would no more think of themselves as being party to soccer violence than my mother would. Much the same thing can be said of Chelsea and the notorious Headhunters. Many people, including a good number of ex- and active hooligans from the West London club, deny that this group ever really existed at all. Yet the name, thanks largely to the media, it must be said, has become synonymous with both the soccer club and the issue of violence among its supporters.

Yet it should be noted that every firm on the list has members who will happily indulge in violence should the opportunity arise. There may be two thousand of them, there may be only twenty, but if you walk around a corner and there they are, the harm they can cause and the damage they can do are immense. Believe me, when you're lying by the side of the road battered and bruised, it doesn't matter one iota who did it, because it still hurts exactly the same.

What follows is a brief selection of the firms together with an explanation as to the origins of their names. The reminder of the list can be found in the Appendix at the back of this book.

Arsenal—The Gooners: Derived from the club nickname the Gunners, the name came into popular use after fans of their local rivals, Tottenham, labeled the Arsenal fans "Goons." So to stop this they adopted the name for themselves.

Birmingham City—Zulu Army: One of the first mixed-race soccer gangs. The chant "Zulu"— made famous in the Michael Caine film of the same name—was first heard being sung by the Birmingham hooligans while playing at Manchester City in 1982.

Bradford City—The Ointment: So called because one would often require medical treatment, including ointment, after encountering them.

Bristol Rovers—The Gas: Took their name from the gasworks next to their original stadium.

Cardiff City — Soul Crew: Originates from a love of soul music.

Chelsea—Headhunters: They hunt for heads!

Manchester United—Red Army: Manchester United play in red, and there are thousands of fans who support them!

Millwall—The Bushwackers: Taken from the Confederate guerrillas who would ambush their enemies during the American Civil War.

Portsmouth—The 657 Crew: Named after the time of the train supporters traditionally took to away games.

Sheffield United—BBC: The Blades Business Crew took their name from the fact that Sheffield was once home to the British steel industry and, therefore, where most of the nations knives —or blades— were made.

Tottenham—The Yids: Derived from the notion that Tottenham has a large Jewish element among its support. The fans adopted the term for themselves to avoid it being thrown at them as a form of anti-Semitic abuse.

West Ham United—ICF: The Inter City Firm, so called because they used the Inter City rail network to get to games.

Wolves—Subway Army: So called because they would often ambush visiting fans in a subway near the stadium.

CHAPTER FOUR

- -

The Early Years

We're here!

No one should make the mistake of thinking that violence involving spectators at soccer games is a relatively new phenomenon because it most certainly is not. I have been researched this issue and have discovered that although the game of soccer appears to have evolved into its modern form in the 1840s, it previously had had a long and bloody history of trouble involving its supporters.

The medieval version of the game, where participants tried to move a leather bag filled with air between defended areas, was so violent that in 1365 King Edward III actually banned it in England. He feared that the rivalries being stirred up would lead to civil unrest. Public records also show that the city of Manchester tried to ban the sport in

1608 due to the mayhem caused by "a company of lewd and disordered persons," whatever that means.

Such things continued as the game evolved and, by the time the version of soccer the world came to know and love was delivered to an eager public in the mid-nineteenth century, trouble involving supporters was fairly commonplace in England. This continued until the beginning of World War I when, due to the war's devastating effect on the male population, England saw a significant dip in the level of violence at games. This pattern continued through the interwar years and up until after the end of World War II.

Every so often, however, crowd violence would resurface with some very ugly occurrences indeed. Millwall, for example, suffered four ground closures between 1934 and 1950, the last one as a result of a two-hundred strong mob that almost beat a match official to death because he made a series of decisions that cost them a game against Exeter City. Despite incidents such as this, interest in soccer increased dramatically in the postwar years. Crowds were up as more and more women began attending games, but crowd control continued to be carried out by only a small number of officers. All that began to change in the mid-1950s when Britain began to go into steady economic and social decline. The boom most people had expected following victory over the Nazis failed to materialize, and the British Empire was beginning to break up. If that wasn't bad enough, in 1956 Britain was drawn into a very nasty conflict regarding the Suez Canal.

These factors seemed to contribute to an increase in juvenile crime. By the early 1950s gangs of teenagers were regularly fighting not just with each other but also with the police. Among these were gangs whose members wore a special style of clothing: a long jacket with velvet collar and cuffs and straight-legged trousers reminiscent of the style worn during the reign of King Edward VII (1901–10). On September 23, 1953, the newspaper the *Daily Express* labeled them "Teddy Boys," after the king. The name stuck.

The effect the Teddy Boys had on soccer was immense. Large numbers of them attended games actively looking for trouble, and the movement was wholly to blame for a significant increase in violence at games in the late 1950s and early '60s. In addition to trouble at the matches, the wholesale destruction of property by these gangs became a serious problem. Trains were a particular favored target as the fans began to travel more freely. This phenomenon in turn led to an increase in the reporting of soccer violence, and it was within such reports that the widespread use of a term that was to become synonymous with the problem first began. The label originated from an Irish immigrant family who terrorized the East End of London in the nineteenth century.

The name of Hooligan, or Houlihan, depending on your research, had settled into history.

By 1962, as the cult of the Teddy Boys had begun to die off to be replaced by two rival youth groups, the Mods—who wore sharp suits, rode motor scooters, and listened to soul and R&B music—and the Rockers—who rode motorbikes, wore leather, and listened to rock and roll—the amount of violence at soccer, although alarmingly high compared to a decade before, had leveled off. Yet the serious social disorder caused by the Mods and Rockers—largely at English seaside towns on national holiday weekends but also at dance halls up and down the country—led the media to increasingly link their activities to those of the soccer fans on a Saturday afternoon. This link was not in fact that strong, as both groups were far more obsessive about bikes, music (and in the case of the Mods, clothes), and beating the crap out of each other than they were about soccer. Largely as a result of this misinformed media coverage, copycat gangs of soccer fans began to spring up all over the country. Slowly, trouble began to spread, and from this point on everything began to change.

Oddly, one of the most significant events in the growth of hooliganism seems to have been the televising of the 1962 World Cup in Chile. Almost for the first time, English soccer fans were able to witness firsthand exactly how other countries' supporters got behind their teams. The singing in particular was a revelation and highlighted the fact that fans could play a more active role in the match day process. Within weeks, supporters up and down the country had formed groups of their own. More important, they had begun to congregate in specific areas of their home grounds and claim them as their own. Primarily, these were behind the favored goal, which is how the concept of ends as we know it today was born. By all accounts, this was *the* place to be on match days back then, and with fans finally able to contribute to game the whole nature of supporting changed. What's more, because on the whole the ends were good-natured places, initially, trouble was rare. But from within the singing groups sprang an element who were "leaders" rather than "followers" and, looking back now, it is easy to see why the ends became such a target later on. After all, segregation of fans was all but nonexistent at that time, largely because it wasn't really required. With many young men wanting to be a part of this new breed of soccer fan, the home ends at most grounds were packed solid.

The year 1963 was significant not just for soccer but for young British men in general. It was the year that marked the end of compulsory military service in Britain. I cannot imagine how much of a relief that must have been to anyone facing two years in the army. The end of conscription marked a major change in British society. Suddenly the old values of respect, compassion, and humility, staple elements of military life, took on less importance. For the youth, the last link with the old way had been removed and rebellion was in the air. Nowhere was that more visible than at soccer games. With money in their pockets and cheaper, faster, and reliable transport more easily accessible, a sharp increase in the numbers of traveling fans—and therefore trouble—was inevitable.

Despite the rising amount of violence among the fans, the average crowd was still regarded as decent and law-abiding. In October 1965, the *Times of London*, together with a number of other newspapers, suggested that English clubs be withdrawn from European competition until the game on the other side of the English Channel had sorted out its hooligan problems. In a cruel twist of fate, however, those words were to come back to haunt the press within days when an incident took place that shook not only soccer but also the country.

Since their formation in 1885, London team Millwall FC had forged for themselves a reputation as a rough club with an even rougher set of supporters. By 1965 that reputation was firmly entrenched among the most notorious in English soccer, and on their travels, especially around the other London clubs, the fans were fearless. When the team traveled to Brentford in West London on November 6, 1965, no one could foresee the effect that their actions that day would have on the future of soccer.

I have talked to many people about this particular game and have also read numerous reports, many of which contradict one another. Indeed, if everyone who claimed to have been there actually had been there, then the stadium must be bigger than I remember it. The simple facts are these: At some point during the game, a hand grenade was thrown from the terrace holding the Millwall fans and bounced onto the pitch. The fact that it was a dud was certainly not known by the players, who must have shit themselves. Well, wouldn't you if a grenade dropped at your feet?

Inevitably, the papers went ballistic, and with the World Cup being staged in England the very next year, the press suddenly altered the way they were reporting upon the behavior of supporters. Suddenly, fans weren't just hooligans, they were thugs and animals. The problem was that at that time the tabloid newspapers in England were involved in a major circulation battle and, as it does now, soccer violence sold papers. As a result, reports and photographs became even more dramatic and headlines more sensationalistic. "Smash the Thugs," "Birch Them!," and even "Cage the Animals" all screamed from the front pages at various times.

Up to that point, most incidents of soccer hooliganism had involved clubs that were fairly local to each other. Traveling long distances was still fairly arduous by train, and for many supporters from the northern clubs visits to London were usually twenty-four-hour affairs. Increasingly, fans were making such efforts, and among that number were a significant number who were on the lookout for trouble. Each week the terraces were alive with talk about who went where, who did what, and what the visiting team would bring with them. In the main, it was little more than bullshit, because each time a tale was told it was embellished to the point that the final version bore no relation to reality. Yet the truth is that no club, with the possible exception of Millwall at Brentford, had ever really done anything that would today be considered out of the ordinary. There had been plenty of battles between fans, of course, but nothing that really had the papers foaming at the mouth. Everything changed in May 1967, however, when an incident took place that rocketed hooliganism to a whole new level.

The clubs with the most notorious followers in 1967 were Millwall, West Ham, and Chelsea. These three teams are all from London, and their geographic proximity meant that they had more local derbies and therefore, more opportunity for violence. The club with the largest support in the entire country, however, was Manchester United. They had a huge fan base in the south of England, and every time the team came to London they attracted massive crowds. Generally, the fact that there were so many of them meant that trouble was minimal because they simply swamped the grounds as well as the surrounding areas. When they came to East London needing to win at West Ham to secure the championship everything changed.

United brought thousands upon thousand of fans with them for the game and basically took over East London. Fighting broke out early on around the ground as the West Ham fans, feeling somewhat put out, tried to regain some of their lost pride. United won the game 6–1 and therefore took the championship, but the day was far from over. Streaming out of Upton Park, the celebrations began. More trouble erupted and the thousands of United fans simply began to trash the surrounding area. It was many hours before calm was restored, but for the West Ham fans it was a crushing and humiliating day. Over the next few weeks, word of this invasion spread like wildfire through the terrace grapevine and suddenly United was being held up as the worst hooligan group in the county. People still claim to this day that following this incident they held that position for the next ten years.

The East End invasion also sparked another problem for both soccer and the police as supporters up and down the country began to look for ways of enhancing their own particular reputations for hooliganism. Liverpool, Leeds, Portsmouth, and even smaller clubs such as Aldershot began to experience serious trouble in and around their grounds on a weekly basis. Much of this was because travel was now easier than it had ever been as a result of the growing use of the "soccer specials."

Originally, clubs had used buses to drive players to grounds for away games. When the demand from families and friends looking to accompany the teams became more pressing, teams began to hire private carriages and use the railways. As the numbers of supporters wanting to travel also increased, the clubs took to hiring whole trains, called soccer specials. Initially, these were simply a means of transport but, over the years, they were to evolve into something that many people, myself included, regard as one of the highlights of their supporting lives.

It is hard to describe the experience of being on a soccer special but I can honestly say that we used to have a blast on ours. Why wouldn't we? A trainload of fellow Watford lads on their way to soccer? It was like a cross between the bar and the terrace.

When I first began to ride these trains, British Rail would always give us the old-style carriages with separate eight-seat compartments and a corridor along one side. This meant that sometimes we'd spend entire trips attacking or being attacked by lads in other compartments. Nothing serious—well, most of the time it wasn't—but a great laugh and a great way to kill the time. Other lads would derive a lot of pleasure from throwing potato chip bags full of urine (or worse!) out of windows as we passed through train stations at speed. I recall that on one trip to Ipswich, we tied this bloke to the luggage rack and left the little twat there while we went to the game. As you can imagine, he was not a happy geezer when we got back, especially as he'd been left hanging upside down.

Another time we were on our way north to Bolton near Manchester, and during the journey we'd been doing the usual fan-spotting and floodlight-watching stuff and were starting to get apprehensive about the game. As usual, when we approached Wigan station near Manchester, the train began to slow down and we all started moaning. Trains always stopped for ages at Wigan in those days, but no one ever bothered to tell us why. This time, however, we stopped on the bridge overlooking the main high street rather than in the station itself. We all jumped up to start slinging abuse at the poor northerners doing their shopping below. When we stuck our heads out of the window we saw the most beautiful sight.

Down below us were about four hundred Manchester City fans who were being held by the police before being escorted to Springfield Park to see their game with Wigan. We started giving them loads of verbal and they gave us loads back. Then someone threw a few toilet rolls, which pissed them off a bit, so the next thing we know one of our lot grabbed a light bulb from its socket and threw that down on them. It was closely followed by almost every bulb on the train and then by all the metal rods from the bottom of the window blinds as well. The City fans went totally apeshit and were running in every direction to avoid the shower. The coppers were freaked because they didn't know what to do either, but they were soon occupied in stopping the City fans coming back up into the station to get to us. The best thing for us, of course, was that we knew these wankers couldn't have a go back and we had a great view of them going mad and fighting with the police.

For once the train started again quite quickly and so the police had no time to pull us off, although I think they were a bit busy controlling the lads in the High Street to worry about us in any case. To this day, whenever I see a City fan, I still have a little chuckle at what we did to them that night. The best thing about the specials was arriving at your destination. That was the real buzz. Pulling in to a station and pouring off the train onto the platform in full song as lines of policemen and local hooligans look on. We're here!

The specials did have a darker side, though. On certain routes the trains would have bricks thrown at them as they passed through stations or sidings, which meant that occasionally you'd have to complete the journey with no windows in your compartment. Some trains would arrive home all but wrecked as the traveling fans had simply taken out their frustration on them after a defeat.

Initially, when their use became widespread in the late 1960s, the specials were a godsend to the police, for they allowed them to exercise strict controls over the movement of supporters around the country. In truth, the control on the trains had little effect on the activities of the hooligans, as there was still no segregation inside grounds. More worryingly, from within the traveling groups emerged a specific but very loose kind of hierarchy. The London clubs in particular were well known for having leaders who called the shots whenever anything happened and, in their own way, these leaders, as I've mentioned, became as famous (or infamous) among the supporters as any of the players.

As hooligan activity continued to increase and media interest in the activities of the gangs grew, crowds began to decline at an alarming rate. As a result, the image of the game seemed to take a battering week in and week out. It must have been difficult back then to comprehend that things could get any worse for soccer, yet this was only the beginning. In the late sixties, a new element was to enter the equation, the skinheads.

Much has been written about the skinhead culture and the simple truth is that it was about three things: music, clothes, and fighting. Furthermore, the one thing the original skinheads were not was racist. After all, ska and reggae, which was their favored music, originated in Jamaica and was brought to Britain by immigrants around 1968. By 1969, the golden year for skinhead culture, soccer had become a natural environment for all those who were into the skin scene.

The skinhead's involvement in, and influence on, soccer was major. The unique style of dress captured the imagination of the tabloid newspapers which loved the idea of something different. Black Harrington jackets, Ben Sherman shirts, Levi's jeans, and Doc Marten boots— all pressed or polished to perfection. The haircut, once described as half soldier, half convict, with nicely shaved sideburns, added to the look. Skinheads looked awesome but they were also bloody terrifying.

Their love of fighting and their "we don't give a fuck" approach to life manifested itself on game days. It had become almost routine for visiting hooligans to try and take over the end favored by the home fans but now it became a thing of honor not only to take an end but also to protect your own. It was, in effect, turf war and thus tailor-made for the skinheads. It is easy to dismiss all this as childish nonsense now, but it took a great deal of nerve to walk onto a rival's end, and it wasn't something to be done if you had no stomach for a fight.

There were various ways of taking an end. If visiting fans got into the stadium early enough, they would already be waiting when the locals arrived and fighting would start almost immediately. If they got there late, it was simply a matter of sneaking into the home end and waiting until they either were spotted by the home support or announced their presence by bursting into song or celebrating a goal with more than the usual vigor. Then all hell would break lose.

The first visible sign of trouble was usually the opening up of a large, gaping hole in the crowd. Around the edges would stand the rival groups, and every so often one would rush forward, lashing out at anyone who came within touching distance with boots or fists before being pushed or pulled back. Within a few seconds, the other group would respond and attack in the same manner and so it would continue. It sounds daft now, but often it was incredibly violent and was certainly very dramatic to watch.

I have to admit, the very first time I ever threw a punch at soccer was during such an incident. A group of lads had tried to take the Watford end, and as I watched, a mere fourteen years old, the pushing and shoving came ever closer until this guy was there right next to me. Someone lashed out at him and, without thinking, I did likewise. It wasn't the best punch I've ever thrown and I doubt he even felt it since it was one of many raining down on him at the time but it sure as shit made me feel good. Great, in fact. I had finally done my bit!

Once trouble had started, the police would usually come pouring in to sort things out and get the groups apart. The trespassers more often than not would then be led around the pitch to the terracing at the other end of the ground where their mates were standing to greet them like heroes. Not much chance of an arrest in those days. Having said that, it wasn't unknown for the police at some grounds to simply leave visiting hooligans in the home end until they had received a few slaps from the local lads before going in to sort things out. Occasionally, the police would throw you out of the stadium and leave you at the mercy of everyone waiting outside.

While taking over someone's end was the ultimate humiliation and the ultimate result for the victor, for the supporters of smaller clubs even getting onto an end and then giving it a bit of mouth was enough of a result, especially if you had hardly any numbers to back you up.

Sometimes, of course, it all went horribly wrong. Invading groups could find themselves confronted by bigger and stronger mobs or individuals would find themselves cut off from their mates and take serious beatings.

I remember standing on the Red Lion End at Watford one night when a group of opposing fans suddenly announced their presence by bursting into song and then lashing out at anyone who made a move toward them. Pretty soon, a large gap had appeared around them but their plan had backfired and they were clearly getting a bit of a kicking from our lads. As the police battled to get up the packed terrace to sort it out, one of the opposition ran toward me seemingly intent on giving me a slap for some reason. Before anything happened, this old guy standing next to me stepped forward and simply held out his arm, fist clenched, and my would-be attacker ran full-pelt into it, all but knocking himself unconscious. It was bloody hilarious and the sight of his mates having to lead him out as he tried to work out where he was as we all roared with laughter is something I will never forget.

Fighting increased across the country and crowds continued to decline at an alarming rate as non-hooligans decided watching soccer simply wasn't worth the hassle. At Nottingham Forest, for example, the average attendances fell from around 20,000 to nearer 10,000 over just two seasons. In response, the police finally began to tighten up and a heavy security presence could be expected at most games. Similarly, as travel to games by bus increased, so did attacks on vehicles. Following increasing complaints from coach companies, motorcycle escorts began to be given to fans coming by road. Yet at some grounds no such luxury was afforded to those who came by train. Often, fans would be let out at the end of a game at the same time and the visitors were left to run a gauntlet of abuse or worse as they made their way back to the station. When you remember that back then almost any rival fan was fair game and that vandalism was rife, it must have been a horrific experience at some grounds.

For the fans, match days had settled into a fairly predictable pattern: Terrace battles and end taking were still fairly frequent, as was trouble in the streets around grounds. August 24, 1973, brought another low point to the history of hooliganism, the first recorded soccer related killing. Bolton had traveled to the seaside town of Blackpool for what was supposed to be a regular league. With Blackpool fans having invaded Bolton's end the previous season, expectations for some kind of revenge attack were high.

Although the fans were searched for weapons going into the ground and kept apart on the terraces, under the stands, in the toilets, and at the refreshment kiosks, the two sets of rival supporters were somehow able to mingle freely with each other. At halftime, the fighting inevitably kicked off and, during the fracas, someone produced an eight-inch sheath knife. A seventeen-year-old Blackpool fan named Kevin Olsson was stabbed through the heart. The person who had lashed out with the knife was just fourteen years old.

The killing sent shock waves through the game, but it can hardly have been a surprise. Stabbings had become commonplace and the sheer numbers of incidents of trouble in and around grounds was rising at an alarming rate. At the end of the previous season, Manchester United fans had brought shame on the club when four hundred of them had invaded the pitch and forced the game against Manchester

City to be abandoned. What is more, Newcastle was having to play all their home Cup ties behind closed doors because of trouble that had occurred during a Cup tie the previous year. The game had simply had enough. It was time for action.

One of the first steps taken was the decision to cage the fans in, the thinking being that if they wanted to behave like animals they would be treated as such. The law-abiding majority supported the idea of anything that might possibly deal with the growing problem of soccer violence, but the hooligan community merely shrugged its collective shoulders at what they all saw as simply the next stage of the game.

For the clubs and the police the cages proved to be an instant success. No longer were the fighting mobs able to surge from side to side across the ends, nor were those who caused trouble able to run off and lose themselves in the crowd. Now they were trapped. Within weeks, the amount of trouble on ends with this style of fencing reduced markedly.

The erection of these enclosures was significant for another, more specific reason. It proved once and for all that the game had just about given up trying to solve the hooligan problem and had decided to simply contain it instead. Tragically, it was a decision that was to have massive implications in the future as the fences would prove to be a major factor in the deaths of ninety-six Liverpool fans at Hillsborough in 1989.

In 1973, however, no one could foresee any such problems, and buoyed by their success the authorities also began to work harder at keeping rival groups apart inside stadia. Initially, the police adopted a more stringent policy of identifying the club loyalties of those entering grounds. In many instances, this was relatively easy because of the regional accents of supporters, but where this was difficult—in London for example, which had more than ten professional clubs—the police would simply ask mundane questions to prove local knowledge such as "What road do you live in?" or "What school did you go to?" And even "Where's the nearest café to the ground?" These were all thrown at me at some point, and if you're not ready for them it's amazing how quickly you can be caught out. In one instance at Vicarage Road, because I had failed to answer a question correctly, the police were convinced I wasn't a Watford fan and wanted to put me in with the visiting supporters.

At games where trouble was almost inevitable—local derbies being a good example—the authorities also began to adopt an "all-ticket" policy that meant that if you wanted to watch, you would be able to gain entry to the stadium only if you purchased a ticket in advance. This was fine for those who lived local and could go to the ground ahead of time to buy tickets but a pain in the ass for those of us who lived a distance away. No credit cards or online ordering back then.

The effect of the clampdown inside grounds was that, outside, trouble increased. Bars began to replace the traditional ends as the place to hit and protect. The added bonus this provided to the hooligans was that trouble would begin earlier in the day, often long before opening time. Indeed, one of the favored tactics among certain groups at the time was to turn up at the home mob's local and force the owner to open up early. By the time the regulars arrived, the outsiders were already in residence, forcing the regulars to either drive the invaders out by force—which almost always led to the pub being wrecked and them being banned—or simply go to another pub and accept it as a defeat. There was always "later on," after all.

There were, however, other changes afoot for the hooligan culture, and this time they had little to do with soccer. It was all about the music. For some years ska had been central to the scene—to this day, the Chelsea team runs out onto the playing field to the theme from *The Liquidator*—but by 1975 it was, together with the skinhead culture, all but dead. There was a clear void developing and it was filled by soul music, which exploded onto the scene. Now I have to say that I am, at heart, a soul boy. For me, the mid 1970s to late '80s was *the* era for music. The bands, especially some of the British jazz-funk exponents, were brilliant and the concerts awesome. However, if the game thought that the demise of the skinhead culture and the rise of dance music would have an effect on the hooligans, it was right. The problem was, rather than reduce it things got even worse.

The first signs of this came with the growing influence of the extreme right-wing political party, the National Front, at soccer. With black players beginning to make increasing inroads into the game, the right wing saw soccer supporters as an obvious target for recruitment, and soon overtly racist publications such as the *Bulldog* could be found on open sale outside grounds. As increasing numbers of fans, both violent and nonviolent, began to follow this bigoted doctrine, some of them even began to adopt the old skinhead style of dress but with totally clean-shaven heads. The image of skinhead was immediately and irreversibly damaged at that point and for the original skins it must have been a sad end.

It is fair to say that most grounds had a right-wing element at this time but that was more a reflection of British society than anything else. In all honesty, many people became involved in the right-wing scene more because of the fear and shock value it provoked in others rather than any specific political belief they held. That was certainly the case among the lads I went to games with who got sucked into that, and all of them look back on that period with some degree of shame.

By 1976 almost every club in the land had fenced in its fans. Not only that, but the police had begun to trial a new weapon, closed circuit television (CCTV). Initially, cameras, and the dire warnings that accompanied their use—"If you're caught on film, you will be arrested, if not today, maybe next week or next month"—sent shock waves through the hooligan world. Yet, amazingly, legal concerns about using cameras caused a good deal of negative publicity, and at some grounds they were withdrawn. But the hooligans had got the message. Trouble began to decrease even further inside grounds, but it exploded elsewhere.

For the London clubs, the subway had always been used to ambush rival fans but now it took on added significance. Firms actually began to haunt specific stations in the hope of picking up stragglers. West London QPR was well known for violence at Ladbroke Grove station, while Fulham Broadway was a no-go area on match days if you weren't a Chelsea fan. On Saturday nights, Euston station—one of the mainline railway terminals in and out of the capital—would become a battleground as fans of the London clubs scrambled to get there before the northern clubs headed home or the London-based Manchester United firm, the Cockney Reds, returned home. The same can be said of all the mainline stations in the capital, and for visiting supporters it must have been a worrying experience. But trouble wasn't confined to the stations in London; wherever fans had to change trains, problems were likely to kick off.

Other sites for trouble were highway service stations. Indeed, some of the worst tales of violence from that time involve these oases of fuel and refreshment. It was certainly common for busloads of fans from two, three, and even four separate clubs to turn up and run riot before the police could get them loaded up and on their way.

I remember one instance when we were driving to a game and pulled into a service station to find about a hundred lads beating the shit out one another in the car park without a single policeman to be seen. After watching for a while to make sure none were Watford fans, we simply drove out and headed up the road to the next one. The arrival of these so-called thug buses into a service station meant only one thing for the management— all your stock would vanish. Many fans made thieving on their travels a matter of principle in the belief that if you treat us badly, we'll act badly a belief that was rife at that time.

The result of all this was that by the end of 1975, most highway service stations would take soccer buses only if they prebooked their arrival so that the police could be present. Even then they were reluctant. For the police, these were problems they did not need. They were also becoming increasingly aware that whatever they used to combat the hooligans simply would not work. But the one thing they did have on their side was the law. This, coupled with the courts' increasing exasperation with hooligan activity, meant that anyone who lodged a complaint against the police, legitimate or otherwise, had no chance of a sympathetic hearing. To the fans, this meant only one thing, that no matter what happened the police would not be called to account.

In effect, the officers of the law now had free rein at soccer and they began to exploit this power to the full. Any fan who traveled around from the mid-1970s to the mid-1980s knows that the police became the real enemy at that point. To the police, everyone suddenly became a potential hooligan, and the abuse, intimidation, and violence dealt out to fans in the name of law and order was unbelievable. Once the police adopted this approach, soccer fans began to feel demonized, which merely reinforced the hooligans' belief that the police were a natural enemy. As a consequence, things took yet another downward turn.

In 1976, soccer suffered a major body blow with the death of a fan at New Cross station in South London. The fatality happened after three Millwall fans chased two West Ham fans onto a train and a fight had broken out. The West Ham fans managed to force two of the Millwall fans back off and started on the other one as revenge. As he fell to the floor, one of the West Ham fans opened the door on the opposite side from the platform and the other one pushed him out onto the tracks. Unfortunately, he was hit by a train and killed instantly.

So shocked were the authorities by this incident that the chairman of the police federation called on the government to suspend the game for a year to allow everything to calm down. The call was totally ignored. Yet if this fatality was bad news for the game, within months soccer was to receive what up to that point was possibly the worst publicity it had ever had. In 1977 the BBC broadcast a television documentary about Millwall's notorious hooligan following. It is impossible now to overstate the impact this program had on soccer. Thanks to the tabloids, everyone in the country already knew about Millwall fans and their exploits but now they saw what was going on firsthand.

While the documentary exposed the existence of groups such as the Half-Way Liners and F-Troop, the most bizarre thing about the program was the fact that the Treatment were shown wearing light-blue surgical headgear to games. Although it has been suggested many times since that this was simply a joke for the benefit of the cameras, no one was laughing at the time because it was too bloody frightening. Whatever the truth of the matter, the effect of the documentary was that within days almost every group in the land had given itself a name and Millwall had reached new heights of infamy.

Increasingly, in an effort to combat the problem, calls were being made to bring about a return to military conscription, and although these usually came from politicians desperate to get their name in the papers, the idea was beginning to win increasing support. When the realization came that the youth would never accept such a move, and as all of them were potential voters—and many already were—the idea was shelved. As if in celebration of this acknowledgment of their power, Britain's youth saw a rebirth of the skinhead movement, followed by and then the emergence of the punk scene.

If the original skins were hoping for a return to the old ways, then they were in for a rude awakening. The new breed of skins was even more aggressive than their predecessors. What's more, racism ran through the scene like a cancer. Together with the punks, the new skinheads set out to forge an even wider division between young and old with, it has to be said, huge success. In later years, bands such as Sham 69 and the Cockney Rejects latched on to their appeal among soccer fans and began to refer to it in their songs. Many even believe that the Sex Pistols classic "Anarchy in the UK" was written about hooliganism. In reality, punk had little influence on soccer, and after 1977 drugs began to make inroads into the scene until, eventually, punk began to parody itself. However, the skins remained and the hooligan scene continued to grow.

As the seventies drew to a close, it was hard to believe that things could get any worse for soccer. Crowds were still dropping and the hooligan gangs, now sporting names and forming identities for themselves, were causing problems all over the country. As if that weren't bad enough, they were also beginning to export hooliganism with them when English clubs played in Europe. Liverpool, Leeds, and Manchester United had all caused trouble on their travels, and at one point the European authorities expelled United from the Winners Cup competition because of trouble with their fans, although they were reinstated on appeal.

If the 1970s had been bad, the '80s were to be even worse. And it all started with the birth of a movement that, unlike the Mods and the skins, did not adopt hooliganism; the Casuals actually grew out from within it.

CHAPTER FIVE

The Casual Era

Don't fuck with us.

In 1979, newly elected prime minister Margaret Thatcher introduced new policies that not only reduced the role of the state in the economy but fueled a much-needed economic boom in the UK. In many ways, the arrival of the Casual scene, with its confidence and arrogance, encapsulated the "don't fuck with us" attitude that suddenly permeated large sections of Britain, particularly London.

Fans suddenly began to take a keener interest not only in their status on the terraces but in the way they were being perceived by outsiders. Fairly quickly, things began to extend beyond simply what you got up to with your fists and into the way you looked and, particularly, what you wore. Style was everything on the terraces. If you went to soccer wearing the wrong clothing designer label, or even the same clothes you had worn the week before, you became an object of ridicule. Clubs, and even regions, quickly developed set styles or adopted specific labels, and for those in the know it was even possible to work out which club a person followed by what he was wearing. Londoners, for example, always seemed to favor white trainers, or sneakers.

The element of one-up-manship was vital to the scene. Styles seemed to change week in and week out, and a label that was essential one week would be old hat the next. The cost of this clothing was often phenomenal. It was not unusual to blow a week's wages on an outfit or even a single jacket. As a result, a new problem began to materialize, not for the police or even for the game but for the lads themselves, and it quickly became the bane of soccer fans. Quite simply, it was the fashion equivalent of being mugged. This is roughly how it worked.

There you'd be, off on your travels with your mates, dressed in your finest gear of Tacchini track-suit top, Lois jeans, and Adidas Trimm Trab trainers looking and feeling the bollocks. Somehow, you've ended up alone and surrounded by a group of local lads who all like the look of your gear and decide they want it. So either you fight or you give it to them.

The media were slow to pick up on the new style trends, but among the earliest to realize what was happening was a young music journalist named Gary Bushell. He labeled these fashion-conscious youths "Herberts," but this term died out to be replaced by the term "Casuals." Other magazines began to report on the trends as well. There has always been huge debate as to who started this trend. The London clubs, particularly Chelsea, laid claim quite early on, asserting that they had begun to adopt a more "discreet but stylish" form of clothing on the terraces to avoid the attentions of the police. However, as a southerner, it pains me to say it but the strongest claim, at least regarding the wearing of sports clothing, comes from Liverpool.

In the mid-seventies, thanks to the Beatles and various high-profile comedians, the population of Liverpool had forged for itself a reputation of being quick-witted and friendly. However, any soccer fan from the late seventies will know that among the traveling fans of both Liverpool and Everton (and, to a lesser extent, Tranmere Rovers) were also some of the most violent and fearless fighters in the country, with a particular fondness for carrying, and using, carpet knives. They were also renowned for indulging in widespread thieving whenever they were on their travels. Indeed, when Everton came to Watford for the first time in 1983, almost every program seller in the town was robbed. As Liverpool traveled around Europe, fans took to stealing expensive designer clothes on a grand scale not just for themselves but also to sell when they got back.

By the end of 1980 people had begun to notice a new style on the terraces, one that was both smart and apparently respectable. As this practice spread, hooligans from all over England began to actually buy clothes from sports shops as well as golf and tennis clubs, and labels such as Fila, Pringle, Ellesse, Tacchini, Diadora, and Lacoste began to appear. Ironically, this was totally against the whole concept of Casual.

Wearing stolen clothes had always been a kind of "anti-rich" statement lent added importance by the "self, self, self" doctrine Margaret Thatcher was busily screaming at the nation. As a consequence, buying clothes, or at least paying the full price, was felt by many die-hard Casuals to be simply falling in line with current fashion and, therefore, consumerism.

For those who had money, particularly those from the southeast of England, which had always been the most affluent region in the country, the fact that they were paying for clothes meant something different. To them, it was more a case of "we can afford to pay for clothes so fuck it. If they get messed up in a fight, we'll just go and buy some more."

The trend of wearing designer clothing meant that the wearing of team colors all but stopped dead. This was a major problem for the police, who found themselves with no obvious method of identifying what club individuals or mobs followed. Keeping opposing sides separated on game days became nearly impossible.

As the Casual scene became more entrenched in the game, the hooligans also became more organized. Up to that point, what planning there had been had revolved largely around travel and drinking. Although there were exceptions, fights had, generally speaking, been spontaneous affairs. But firms now began to plan in advance. If phone numbers of rival groups were known, contact would be made and challenges issued. In later years, hooligans even began to use the personal columns in magazines to place ads announcing where they would be and at what time on specific match days. Another development was the increasing use of spotters, young lads who went out actively looking for rival firms and who would then report their whereabouts back to the main group. It was even widely believed that in London, West Ham had a group of lads on scooters who would shuffle information around at an alarming rate.

Sometimes, they didn't need spotters to find you. While walking to West Ham one Saturday, one of our lot thought he'd be clever and walk on the opposite side of the road from where we were being escorted by the police with the other Watford fans. Within about five minutes, he felt a tap on the shoulder and heard a voice in his ear whisper, "We've seen you!" Not surprisingly, he shit himself and was soon back among us where he should have been.

Travel was another thing that began to change with

groups of casuals traveling more independently of the normal supporters to avoid the attentions of the police. This meant that the use of trains, with the inevitable police presence, declined rapidly and that journey by road increased significantly. Minivans, or as they later became known "battle buses," would travel in convoy and carry formidable firms. A few clubs even adopted more outrageous forms of transport, many of which were designed with only one purpose in mind. I was told years ago that a group of thirty or so Luton hooligans would often travel to games in a large, U-haul-style dump truck and, once they had found the home pub, would simply pull up outside, drop the tail gate, and steam out, attacking anyone and anything before vanishing as quickly as they had arrived.

Tactics varied from club to club. Both Manchester United and Chelsea had so many lads willing to be involved that they would flood areas and grounds and simply invite trouble. Chelsea, in particular, would often leave town after a game and then return two or three hours later to hit the home fans in a pub or club with devastating results. West Ham, on the other hand, still favored infiltration into grounds and had enough lads who had the nerve, or stupidity, to try this tactic everywhere they went. Millwall simply spread fear before them.

Weapons were also coming into increasing use and,

more frighteningly, the hooligans began developing varia-
tions of their own. Millwall, inevitably, had taken the lead
with what was known as the Millwall Brick. Quite simply, it
was made from a newspaper that, when folded in a particular way, becomes as hard as iron. When held in the fist, it is
as good as any knuckle-duster. The beauty of the Millwall
Brick was that it could be constructed quite easily once inside the ground so avoiding detection if you were searched
on the way in. Another weapon that came into use at that
time was the dual-cut Stanley blade. This was simply two
blades taped together with a matchstick in between them.
The resultant cuts, being so close together, were all but impossible to stitch properly, which meant that the scars were
huge. One favorite place for being slashed was across the
backside, because it meant that the victim could not sit
down for weeks or at least until the scars had healed. Other
weapons that saw the light of day at about that time were
golf balls with small slivers of razor blade stuck to them with
superglue, cigarette packets full of rocks, and small nasal
spray bottles full of ammonia that were sprayed into peoples
faces. Some firms even used to fill their pockets with marbles
or ball bearings. When things kicked off and the mounted
police turned up, these would be rolled along the road in
front of the horses causing serious problems as the animals
are unable to walk on such small, hard objects.

Personally, maybe because I spent the working week in a military environment geared to the idea of killing as many people as possible, I abhorred the use of weapons at soccer and I still do. To me, fighting is about fist and boot, period. Still, I certainly wasn't averse to throwing stuff back if it was thrown at me, though. Fuck that!

Yet another murder occurred in 1982. The impact it had on the game was immense, for it marked a new and sinister development. When an Arsenal fan was found stabbed to death after a game with West Ham, the police were amazed to find that pinned to his chest was a business card on which were the words "Congratulations, you've just met the ICF."

Inevitably, press coverage ensured that within days firms up and down the country were having their own cards printed, often on machines handily located in train stations that could turn out 150 cards for only five dollars. People even began collecting them, and to this day they pop up every so often on eBay. Even as the clamor for action to curb the continuing hooligan problem began to gather pace, the nation was rocked by an even bigger dilemma, one which I have touched on a couple of times already—the Argentinean forces invasion of the Falkland Islands.

The impact of war on Britain was unbelievable. Suddenly, the nation had a single and very real enemy. One which quickly became a focus for a rash of xenophobic hatred as patriotism, for so long a dirty word under the previous socialist government, spread though the population like wildfire.

Some academics even began to voice the idea that the terraces might finally see a decline in hooligan activity as the nation became unified behind our troops and a common goal. No chance.

The mayhem showed no signs of easing up. As firms sought to enhance reputations, hits and ambushes became even more daring and organized. One of the most famous of these inevitably involved Millwall, whose reputation as being the worst of all hooligan groups was firmly established, and Bristol City, one of the few rival groups who regularly beat them. From this developed a feud that ranks among one of the most intense of all time.

It began in 1983 when Bristol City's mob traveled to the capital and wrecked one of Millwall's main bars. In revenge, later that season the Londoners traveled to Bristol and caused mayhem. They warmed up by wrecking a pub three miles from the ground, then they staged a series of attacks on the home club's main bars. During the various incidents, a number of local supporters were stabbed and one ended up with a broken back. Eventually, the City mob got themselves organized and fought back. They attacked any Millwall fans they could find; one incident occurred where two fans were grabbed and thrown off a bridge onto some railway tracks below.

When the home fans finally made their way into the ground, they found that Millwall had infiltrated just about every section. Not surprisingly, trouble broke out almost immediately, and the police struggled for control.

A few weeks after this, with no game of their own to go to, a small group of City fans decided to take revenge for the broken back suffered by one of their lads. They "liberated" the large wooden sign from one of the bars that had been wrecked by the Millwall hooligans, jumped in some cars, and began the hundred-mile journey to London. At 2:30 a.m., having sprayed "BCFC" on the sign, they pulled up outside a packed-solid Millwall pub and hurled it through the window before jumping back in their cars and driving off.

Not surprisingly, the Millwall hooligans were furious and decided that they would finish this feud once and for all. And when it came, the attack was on a scale rarely if ever seen before. In early 1985, the next time Bristol City played Millwall, the supporters' buses heading for the ground found themselves directed by traffic signs down a dead-end road some nine miles from the ground. Waiting for them were approximately one hundred Millwall hooligans, who launched a ferocious attack that left every single coach wrecked and a large number of people injured.

The planning and precision of this hit was almost military, and it worked perfectly. More important, the reputation of the Millwall fans as being fearless was at a new height. Incredibly, it reached an even higher plane just a few months later when, in March, they traveled to Luton's Kenilworth Road stadium and rioted in full view of the television cameras.

If the eighties had been bad up to that point, 1985 was, and remains, the worst year for soccer violence. The trouble at Luton remains possibly the most highly publicized incident of hooliganism ever seen. Inevitably, since it had been largely dependent on achieving a reduction in hooligan activity, the English FA's offer to stage the European Championship Tournament in 1988 was finished as soon as the first seat was ripped up and thrown, but more worryingly for the game, the government went mad. Soccer's governing bodies were immediately summoned to explain themselves to Margaret Thatcher. Unfortunately, they told her that hooliganism wasn't a soccer problem at all; it was society's problem. Therefore, it had nothing to do with the game and any resolution could come only via the government. Given that she had never been a fan of the game and had always expressed anger at the damage the hooligans had done to England's reputation over the years, one can only guess at this formidable woman's reaction to this abdication of responsibility, but immediately she instructed her government to draw up plans for a national ID system for soccer fans. For good measure, she also forced through a ban on the sale of alcohol at matches.

On May 11, 1985, the same day that fifty-six soccer fans died in a fire caused by a burning cigarette under the wooden grandstand at Bradford City's stadium, Leeds United fans ran riot at Birmingham City's ground. Injured that day were ninety-six policemen, and a young boy was killed when a wall collapsed as supporters were being crushed against it trying to escape the fighting. The nation went into shock. Even though the Bradford fire had nothing to do with hooliganism, there was a very real sense even among the Casual community that things had gone too far. Soccer is, after all, only a game.

Just eighteen days later, that same game was to suffer what was almost a fatal body blow when Liverpool fans caused the deaths of thirty-nine Italian soccer fans when they charged across a terrace at Heysel Stadium in Belgium.

That Heysel was a tragedy is beyond question but although condemnation of the Liverpool fans was swift, things were not as simple as they first appeared. Indeed, like all such things, the tragedy was the culmination of events that had actually begun a year prior to this game

In 1984, having made it to their fourth European Cup final, Liverpool and its many thousands of traveling supporters journeyed to Italy looking to build on what was already a formidable reputation as one of the all-time great teams. Unlike previous occasions, this time they went as underdogs, for the game was to be played in Rome and on the home pitch of their opponents, A.S. Roma.

Inevitably, with so much at stake for the local side and a support that outnumbered them by many, many thousands, the reception given to the Liverpool fans was less than welcoming. As Liverpool fans entered the stadium, stewards and policemen confiscated coins, bunches of keys, watches, and even cameras, which if anything fueled a degree of hostility among the Liverpool support especially when they soon came under attack from a hail of missiles.

Despite the obvious tension inside the ground, the English side went on to win the game in a penalty shoot-out, but even as the players celebrated on the pitch things on the terraces began to take a very nasty turn. Almost immediately, the police became openly hostile toward the Liverpool fans and it quickly became clear, especially to the seasoned travelers, that there would be trouble outside the ground. What no one expected was that it would be quite as bad as it was.

While some of the Liverpool support managed to make their way to the center of the city to be pictured dancing in the famous Trevi Fountain, others headed for their hotels and supposed safety. However, they soon found themselves the targets of local youths who seemed totally indifferent to the fact that many of the English supporters were family groups, some of which included quite young children. Worryingly, the police seemed unsympathetic to the plight of the English and, in many cases, actually became a part of the problem by lashing out at the English fans as they pleaded for protection. Inevitably, the situation deteriorated. Gangs of youths on motor scooters began chasing the Liverpool fans along narrow streets and slashing out at them with knives as they rode past. In one horrific incident, a thirteen-year-old was almost hacked to death and required two hundred stitches to his head alone.

To make matters worse, coach drivers who had been due to take some of the Liverpool fans to the Rome airport after the game simply went home, leaving the fans stranded and at the mercy of the roving gangs. Some hoteliers, whether in fear for their premises or resentment at the result, refused entry to their English guests, some of whom were forced to seek sanctuary in the British embassy.

It was a shameful episode and the fact that it received so little media attention in either Italy or England caused outrage among the Liverpool support as well as in the greater English hooligan community. Revenge was sworn and, only a year later, the opportunity to take it arrived when the team, having made it to the European Cup final yet again, discovered that they were heading for Belgium to face another Italian side, Juventus.

Leaving aside the simmering tensions, how or why the Heysel stadium was chosen to host this fixture is something of a mystery. Having been condemned many times for failing to meet even the very basic of modern safety standards, a lack of maintenance meant that large sections of the ground were crumbling and covered in knee-high weeds. Security even for domestic games was regarded by the locals as something of a joke. For a fixture of this stature it was simply laughable.

Ironically, the Liverpool fans arrived in Brussels in a subdued mood as a result of the shock caused by the Bradford fire, and for the vast majority trouble was the last thing any of them wanted. Sadly, their mood didn't last. Violence erupted in various parts of Brussels during the day as Liverpool fans, many veterans of the game in Rome, once again found themselves the target of Italian hooligans, this time in the shape of the Juventus Ultras.

However, on this occasion the Liverpool fans were ready and fought back. The hooligans among them took the Italians' aggression as a sign that they wanted a continuation of the trouble from the previous year. If the Italians wanted it, Liverpool had plenty of lads in Brussels who were more than capable of providing it. Payback had been handed to Liverpool on a plate.

Despite this assertion, the Liverpool fans did not immediately go on the offensive. Instead, they settled into the cities bars and responded where necessary until the Belgian police, who seemed totally unprepared for what was happening, eventually decided that, rather than arrest or detain people, the best tactic was to get the fans into the ground as quickly as possible. This was to prove a huge mistake for one simple reason: segregation.

The ticketing situation had been a shambles from the start. Many of those who had bothered to buy tickets from official sources found themselves separated from the Italians by a flimsy fence and a few disinterested stewards. Others, who had brought theirs locally or had simply gotten into the ground by climbing under, over, or even through the perimeter fencing ended up spread around the terraces. As a result, segregation was almost nonexistent and with over two hours to go in a stadium full of some of the most embittered supporters the game has ever seen small pockets of Liverpool fans soon began to gather together.

Ironically, it was the Italian fans who kick-started the trouble inside the ground and the bulk of the Liverpool fans, who were gathered together on one half of the large western terrace, came under attack from a barrage of bottles, coins, and flares. This quickly escalated into direct violence as Juventus supporters began attacking groups of Liverpool fans located in other areas of the ground. As the Liverpool fans fought back, and with the police seemingly unable or unwilling to take control, these small skirmishes rapidly escalated into large terrace battles.

At approximately 8:45 p.m., a section of the Liverpool support on the western terrace decided enough was enough and forced their way through a fence and charged at the mass of Juventus fans who had been hurling a steady stream of missiles at them. Immediately, panic set in among the Italians, who turned and fled. However, with the other three sides of the terrace surrounded by a concrete wall, they simply had nowhere to go.

The Liverpool fans, seemingly unaware of what was happening on the far side of the terrace they were attacking, continued to drive forward at the Juventus supporters, who by now were desperately climbing over each other in an effort to escape. As the police were still trying to work out what to do, the inevitable happened and the crumbling wall at the eastern end of the terrace collapsed. The release of pressure sent the helpless Italians who had been crushed against it tumbling to the ground. Even as they lay there, the remainder of the Juventus support poured through the gap, crushing their fellow supporters underfoot.

As the rest of the spectators witnessed the tragedy unfolding, all hell broke loose. Italian fans in other parts of the ground invaded the pitch in an effort to get at the Liverpool support and, at one point, it even appeared that a Juventus supporter was firing a gun into the English section (it later turned out to be a starting pistol). With the situation now seemingly out of control, the Belgian police were finally spurred into action, and when reinforcements arrived, supplemented by units from the Belgian army, order was quickly restored.

Incredibly, despite the deaths of thirty-nine Italian fans and with neither set of players wanting to take play, the decision was made that the game had to go ahead. The reasoning was that, if it didn't, the fans would cause even more mayhem in the streets of Brussels. In one of the most controversial games in the history of soccer, Juventus won the 1985 European Cup final 1–0. But the result was meaningless.

Because the game was broadcast live, pictures of the disaster were seen around the world, and, inevitably, every ounce of blame fell on the Liverpool fans. The Belgian authorities, in a desperate but ultimately flawed damage-limitation exercise, accused the Englishmen of being "fighting mad" and told of one who had to be injected with enough tranquilizer to knock out six horses before he would calm down. There was even talk that those held in custody would be charged with mass murder.

Almost immediately, rumors began circulating that among the Liverpool fans had been known hooligans from a variety of clubs including Chelsea, Newcastle, West Ham, Millwall, and Leeds. Desperate for a new angle on the hooligan issue, the tabloid press in England jumped on these rumors and informed the world that Heysel had actually been a planned show of strength by the English hooligan elite as revenge for the events in Rome the previous year. It was also claimed that it had been a group of Chelsea fans that had kicked everything off. In all the research I have done on this incident, no one has ever provided a shred of evidence that supports this claim. Where the rumors came from is still unclear, but given that the club has always enjoyed a wealth of support from across the whole of England, it is possible that there were Liverpool fans from all over the country in Brussels and the different regional accents heard at the time have more to do with that than any half-baked theory. Indeed, many Liverpool fans I have spoken to who were at Heysel angrily refute the suggestion that it was a planned show of strength by several firms and make it plain that this was very much their fight alone and that it was one they wanted.

Ironically, I was actually on a military exercise in Belgium on the night of the Heysel disaster. And, to make matters worse, I was the only Englishman among almost a hundred Belgian, Italian, German, and Scottish servicemen watching the tragedy unfold live on TV. Although no one said anything to me directly, it was clear from the glances in my direction that, having been openly supporting Liverpool throughout the day, I was being held guilty by association. As a result, I left without a word before the game kicked off. It was the only time in my life I have ever been embarrassed to be English.

Not surprisingly, within days of the incident, English clubs were banned from European competition indefinitely, with Liverpool having a further three-year ban on top of that. Incredibly, four of the five English clubs that had qualified to play in Europe the following season challenged this ban in the High Court, claiming it was unfair because it had nothing to do with them. Thankfully, the courts upheld the decision.

Within the hooligan community, Heysel was a huge wakeup call as there was a sudden realization about exactly what, and how much, was at stake. I mean, this was murder on a grand scale and it was all so bloody pointless. Unbeknownst to the hooligans changes were afoot. While they had been causing havoc around the country, the police had finally decided to smash the organized groups once and for all. They went undercover.

Astonishingly, close-knit hooligan groups at Chelsea, Millwall, Birmingham Leeds, Luton, and numerous others were infiltrated by undercover officers. Ringleaders from clubs across the country were arrested, charged, and in most cases, imprisoned. Once the police had shown their hand and news of the undercover operations broke, the impact on hooligans throughout the country was major. After all, if Chelsea, known as one of the closest-knit groups in the land, could be infiltrated by the police, what chance would most of the others have? The government had also gone on the offensive with yet more legislation and this, together with the increasing use of closed circuit TV at games, proved once and for all that hooliganism was being taken seriously. Almost immediately, there was a sharp decline in trouble at games and, although it didn't solve the problem completely, for the first time things began to look promising.

Outside of soccer, the organized side of hooliganism was still something of a mystery. In 1988, however, a film was released that exposed the "reality" of the hooligan groups. *The Firm*, with a brilliant cast led by Gary Oldman, was very much a product of its time, and for the first time, the brutality of hooliganism was laid bare for all to see as was the sheer folly of it all. Although dated now, it is possibly the best of all the hooligan movies.

As the game moved through the 1987–88 season, the number of reported incidents continued to decline and the European championships in Germany were played relatively peacefully. The reason, in part, was the emergence of a new culture that was becoming increasingly attractive to young men all over Britain, the rave scene.

The attractiveness of the dance scene at that time cannot be underestimated. Not only did it involve the obvious combination of music, dance, and women, it also included a slightly subversive element. Illegal raves in warehouses and fields often involved traveling around the country to stay one step ahead of the police, and this must have been incredibly exciting. What is more, the explosion of illegal drugs that surrounded this scene also had a major impact on hooliganism. If you were doped up to the eyeballs, the last thing you wanted to do was fight anyone. On the face of it, things were looking up and the government was quick to laud the success of the anti-hooligan measures it had taken since the dark days of 1985.

The Casual scene had also gone through something of a change with the arrival of clothing brands that became almost synonymous with the cult. Stone Island, characterized by its trademark compass badge on the sleeve, had become essential wear to the extent that on match days, certain bars would place "No Stone Island" signs in the windows because they knew that lads wearing them were potentially trouble.

But as April 1989 approached, despite a certain cooling down of trouble, the police reaction to soccer fans was unchanged. Everyone was a potential hooligan and all were to be treated as a possible threat. Then came the event that changed everything.

To negate any potential home advantage, semifinal games for the FA Cup competition are traditionally held at a neutral venue, with the final being held at Wembley Stadium in London. When Liverpool and Nottingham Forest qualified for the latter stages in 1989, the venue chosen was one widely regarded as one of the best soccer stadiums in England at that time, Hillsborough Stadium in Sheffield.

As kickoff time approached, a crush developed in the streets outside the Leppings Lane end of the stadium as upwards of 5,000 people tried to get in. To relieve the pressure, the police decided to open a set of double doors that was normally used only as an exit.

Tragically, the number of Liverpool fans pushing through these doors meant that the stewards inside were unable to control the people flooding in and so another crush developed, this time inside the pens behind the goal that were already packed with people waiting for the game to start. As more and more people arrived, the crush became steadily worse, and at 3:06, with the game already under way, people began to climb over the fences to escape.

Believing this to be nothing more than a pitch invasion of the type seen a thousand times before, the police advised the match officials to stop the game and sent on reinforcements to clear the playing field.

By the time they finally realized that something was terribly wrong, people had already lost their lives, with some actually dying from being crushed as they stood upright. By the time it was all over, in what will always be one of the darkest days in world soccer, ninety-six people were dead. Ironically, even as the dead were being dragged from the Leppings

Lane end, the police formed a cordon on the halfway line to stop the Liverpool fans reaching the Nottingham Forest fans who were simply watching, horrified, at the other end of the stadium. Some who tried to break through to ferry the injured to waiting ambulances were forcibly turned back.

Quite rightly, the police have been heavily criticized for their failure to stop the crush in the road outside as well as the decision to open the gates in the first place, but a lot less has been made of the simple truth that if Liverpool supporters without tickets had not been trying to force their way in—as they and others had done a thousand times before and would indeed again as recently as May 2007 ahead of the Champions League final in Athens—those ninety-six souls would still be alive today. Any way you look at it, those people died as a direct result of the threat of hooliganism. If people had not caused trouble in the past, there would have been no need for fences.

Arguments about which end the Liverpool fans should have been in and why a security cordon wasn't in place outside the stadium to make sure the fans going into the ground had tickets are largely irrelevant. All English soccer fans are to blame in part for what happened at Hillsborough because either we played our part in dragging the game down to that point or we simply sat back and watched while others did it. Yes, I am as guilty as anyone.

The subsequent investigation into and resulting report on the Hillsborough disaster changed English soccer forever because it finally forced the game to get its act in gear. The fences came down and all-seater stadia became compulsory in the top divisions of the English league.

Furthermore, Hillsborough was also responsible for something else that was to have a major effect on soccer because there was a sudden realization among both the general public and, more important, the police that not all of the game's supporters were potential hooligans. Some were actually people who simply wanted to watch a game of soccer. The very fact that policemen stood by and watched, convinced that they were seeing just another episode of hooliganism rather than innocent men and women being crushed to death, proves just how jaundiced they had become after years of dealing with soccer violence.

As a result, the police's attitude toward their role changed and from that point on the demonization of supporters died down. There was certainly much less of the in-your-face style of policing to which we had become accustomed.

There was also a realization in the hooligan community that things had simply gone too far. Many lads made the conscious decision to step away from the violence while others stopped going to games altogether, sickened by what had happened at Hillsborough.

As a result, the following season would be one of the quietest for many a year with official arrest figures showing a reduction for the first time in years, a trend that was set to continue with figures for 1990–91 showing a drop of a third from almost 6,000 to a little over 4,000. On the face of it, things were looking up and the government was quick to laud the success of the anti-hooligan measures it had taken since the dark days of 1985.

The figures did not, however, provide an entirely accurate reflection of what was going on for there was a very big fly in the ointment. Even as the first full post-Hillsborough season was drawing to a close, English soccer was packing its collective bags and heading for Italy and the 1990 World Cup finals.

It did not go smoothly.

CHAPTER SIX

The Naughty Nineties

This time, instead of serious wounds,
we had deaths.

The mixture of summer sunshine, English lads, lager, and soccer has always given the authorities reason to worry. When England qualified for the World Cup in Italy in 1990, the British government was determined to finally crack the hooligan nut once and for all. Their plans to thwart the traveling thugs by making it all but impossible for fans to buy tickets in the UK were dashed when the Italians let it be known that tickets would be freely available to anyone throughout the tournament.

With the first of the England games being held on the island of Sardinia, hopes were high that things would be relatively calm. The trouble was, no one told the local youths who seemed intent on dishing out as much grief to the tourists as possible. The result? A brawl involving more than five hundred people during which the Italian police fired live rounds over the heads of the crowd in an effort to quell the violence.

Due to an alcohol ban in Bologna, where the England team was due to play its second game, a large number of England fans had taken up residence in Rimini, some eighty miles away. When Italy beat Uruguay 2–0 to make it through to the quarter-final stage, Italian supporters poured onto the streets to celebrate. The festivities involved hurling abuse at a small group of England fans who, in typical English fashion, replied first with abuse and then with a barrage of missiles. As the situation deteriorated, the police finally arrived and drove the locals away, then told the English lads that they were going to take them back to their hotels for their own safety. Instead, however, they were taken straight to the local airport and flown out of the country.

As a result of the trouble on that one night, 238 people were deported. It was the largest single peacetime deportation in Italian history.

By the time the tournament was over, the total number of deported swelled to more than four hundred. The British government was incensed, yet the Italian authorities congratulated the English fans on their behavior and admitted that the vast majority of those deported were innocent of anything other than overzealous policing. The English media joined in and actually began to praise the supporters. All of this seemed to confirm that English soccer fans were now very different from those who blitzed their way across Europe in the early eighties. The reality is that the group was motivated by exactly the same feelings as before, but now rioting and vandalism seemed to be replaced by drinking and partying. I'm not saying that fans weren't happy to stir trouble, but most often that trouble occurred as a reaction to provocation from locals or the police rather than from planned violence.

Even the sports governing bodies understood this and not only allowed Manchester United and Aston Villa back into European competition but invited England to bid to host the 1998 World Cup. This bid was eventually withdrawn, but only in favor of an ultimately successful bid to host Euro '96. It seemed that the bad times were over and the game moved into the next phase of the post-Hillsborough era with a sense of optimism it hadn't experienced, well, ever.

If English soccer was genuinely beginning to think that hooliganism was a thing of the past, it was only deluding itself. In February 1992, the first serious pitch invasion inside an English ground in years forced the hooligans back onto the front pages of the papers. At Birmingham City, more than two hundred fans invaded the pitch, and one of them attacked the match official after Stoke City had scored a late equalizer.

Eventually, the players were forced to leave the playing field. After the entire stadium had been cleared of supporters, they were brought back on to play out the last thirty-five seconds in front of almost empty grandstands. Incredibly, the Birmingham chairman all but blamed the invasion on the ineptitude of the officials with the result that the authorities hit him with a misconduct charge, fined the club £50,000, and ordered the teams to play two matches behind closed doors.

Soon afterward, Millwall hit the headlines again when, at the last-ever game at their infamous ground the Den, hooligans rioted and almost ripped the place to shreds, just weeks before the bulldozers were due to move in and demolish it. Months later, serious trouble broke out at their new stadium, one specifically designed to thwart hooligan violence, and the Charlton team's chairman was attacked. As if this weren't bad enough, within weeks things would sink to a new low at the club.

Having made the end-of-season playoffs, Millwall played host to Derby County. During the game, horrific racial abuse was poured onto the two black players in the Derby side. So intimidating was the atmosphere that both players were substituted before the end of the game. When the final whistle blew, the Millwall fans invaded the pitch, and in an incident that sent disgust running through soccer, the Derby keeper was attacked. After the game, all hell broke loose with Millwall fans even setting fire to a car from the BBC Derby radio station. Fighting continued on the subway as the Derby fans battled their way back to their trains. The real significance of the melee was possibly the first use of something that was to become an essential tool in later years: the cell phone. Although cell phones were becoming more widely used almost by the week, they were still quite bulky and expensive. During this particular incident, fans on both sides were seen using them to call up reinforcements. From that point on, as they became more available, not to mention smaller, cell phone use by hooligan groups increased markedly.

With this tool at their disposal, the mobs began to become seriously organized and the prearranging of fights became the norm as rival gangs could locate each other almost instantly. The only problem was getting the other person's number, but that could usually be obtained via the hooligan grapevine.

Despite this alarming development, the fact that the trouble was taking place almost entirely away from the stadiums gave the impression that hooliganism was no longer a serious problem. Indeed, by the spring of 1994, after I'd finally taken the plunge and left the air force, I rarely saw anything untoward inside any ground. I heard about it, of course, and the Casuals still roamed the streets bedecked in Stone Island under the watchful eyes of the closed circuit TV cameras, but it was rare to see them in action.

However, a warning of potential problems came from an unlikely source when, in 1994, a video entitled *Trouble on the Terraces* was released. Narrated by *Lord of the Rings* actor Sean Bean and featuring a host of academics, it was supposed to be a serious examination of the hooligan issue. What it actually was, however, was a cynical attempt to make money by showing footage of fights and pitch invasions, and it sold by the truckload. The authorities were furious at what they regarded as the promotion of hooliganism, but if they thought this was a problem it was nothing to what lay ahead. The dark side of English soccer was about to hit the front pages of just about every newspaper in the world.

In January 1995, during an FA Cup tie at Selhurst Park, Eric Cantona, captain of Manchester United and quite possibly the team's greatest player ever, was sent off for a bad tackle during a game against London club Crystal Palace. As he walked off the field, a fan ran down to the touchline and began gesturing and hurling abuse at Cantona who, within seconds, had flown at him with a kung fu–style kick. When this kick failed to connect with the offending fan, Cantona jumped up from the ground where he had fallen and lashed out with his fists before his teammates and various stewards managed to drag him away.

The pictures of the incident were broadcast around the planet and, the next day, the newspapers had labeled Cantona a hooligan and were calling for him to be jailed. So bad did it become that in an attempt to defuse the situation, United immediately banned Cantona for the rest of the season.

Abusing players has always been standard practice among fans and in most instances it is fairly good-natured since it really has one of only two purposes: to make each other laugh or to let a player know what you think of him. Players might not like that, but they understand it just as they know that putting up with it goes with the territory. After all, for the most part your own fans will be supporting you and urging you on but if they're getting on your back it means that they think you're having a shit game, and since they pay your wages they have a right to let you know. Conversely, if the opposing fans are giving you shit, it means you're having a good game and any player worth his salt will feed off that and use it to his advantage.

Sometimes, of course, the nature of the abuse becomes unacceptable because there are some things about which you just don't joke. Not even me. The most high-profile examples of this are the taunts that were aimed at David Beckham shortly after the 2002 World Cup and his dismissal during the game against Argentina when groups of so-called fans were all but wishing cancer on his children. Although he must have been desperate to jump into the crowd and beat the crap out of the people involved, it is to Beckham's eternal credit that he never reacted. Instead he let his performances on the pitch do the talking and for that he remains one of soccer's greats.

Instances of players reacting to abuse used to be quite rare. In fact the only time I ever saw it happen was during an away game at Oxford United where the Watford fans spent the entire game hurling abuse at a player called John Aldridge. Our abuse, however, certainly was justified. Having just agreed on a deal to transfer to Liverpool, to us Aldridge appeared to be going through the motions to avoid picking up an injury, and to any fan, even those of other teams, not trying is the ultimate betrayal. Eventually, Aldridge had simply had enough of us and gave us the finger. All that achieved was to make the abuse even more vitriolic. It also cemented his place in my top-ten most hated players of all time. How dare he abuse me!

These days, players are happy to react to fans' taunts, albeit from a distance. Manchester United's Christian Ronaldo frequently places a cupped hand behind his ear as he runs past opposing fans after scoring a goal and has even been known to place a forefinger over his lips once or twice to tell them to shut up. Still, he is a genius, so fair's fair.

There is one type of abuse that is not only unacceptable, it is now actually illegal, and that is racist abuse. Whenever I talk about or write anything about racism, the first thing that enters my head is a brief flash of a photograph. To be more precise, a specific photograph of one of the greatest players ever to pull on a Watford shirt let alone one of England, and one of the first players I truly idolized, John Barnes.

The picture, taken at the Liverpool versus Everton Merseyside Derby in 1987, is actually quite unremarkable. Barnes is shown resplendent in his typical late-eighties skin-tight kit, seemingly controlling a ball that isn't even in the shot. In any other circumstance, it would have been dumped by the photographer as a nothing picture.

Yet this is no normal circumstance. That picture has become one of the most symbolic sporting photographs ever taken because of what can be seen in the bottom left-hand corner. It is a single banana. Barnes wasn't controlling, he was back-heeling that banana from the pitch. Barnes never made much of it at the time, but in numerous interviews since he has highlighted the fact that bananas, monkey chants, and verbal racist abuse aimed at black players had been the norm for years. As someone who had followed both Barnes and his teammate Luther Blissett around the country for years with Watford, I'd heard them take horrific abuse at certain grounds. In typical Watford fashion, it simply made us raise our game and give them even more vocal support.

By the beginning of the 1990s, thanks to the actions of numerous antiracism groups and with the support of the vast majority of fans, verbal racism seemed to have mostly been eradicated from English soccer. The actions of Eric Cantona dragged racial problems back into the public eye. Within days of his assault on the Crystal Palace fan, Cantona's legal team issued the claim that while there could be no justification for his actions, they were understandable because the fan he had assaulted had been racially abusive. It was a claim that almost certainly saved Cantona from jail. The English media immediately switched sides, and almost overnight Cantona went from being thug to victim. When allegations surfaced that the fan he had assaulted had a history of involvement with extreme right-wing politics, the press were salivating with delight. Then news broke that the guy also had a record of involvement in hooliganism. You could almost hear sports-writers up and down the land orgasming. Once again, head-lines such as "Soccer's Racist Shame" and "Nazi Hooligans Blight Soccer" screamed from the back pages.

In reality, extreme right-wing political groups such as the National Front, the British Movement, and the League of St. George had been involved with English soccer for at least two decades prior to this game and it is easy to see why. After all, where else in the 1970s and '80s did large numbers of primarily working-class males gather together? In the late 1980s, the impact of the political groups declined rapidly, particularly at club level. The England national side, however, continued to be affected by a small presence. Various groups were involved in some shameful episodes on their travels. During a trip to Poland in 1993, for example, some England fans had even been photographed laughing and smiling at the Auschwitz museum.

Every country in Europe had problems of a similar nature but what was unique to England was that the nationalist right-wing groups had a specific and very real focus for their hatred. The singing of "No Surrender to the IRA" had become so ingrained among the English support that it had almost come to be regarded as their theme song. While many ridiculed both it and the people who sang it, the song's continuing presence highlighted the simple truth that loathing for the Irish Republican Army and everything it stood for existed among fans and hooligans alike. As the continuing Anglo-Irish peace process seemingly conceded more and more ground to the IRA, a 1995 game between England and Dublin handed the extreme right wing an ideal opportunity to show its support for the loyalist community in Northern Ireland and to send a warning to the British government that there was a section of the community who were far from happy with what was going on.

On the day of the match, the England fans flooded into Dublin, and although they were extremely loud and very anti-Irish trouble was negligible. Inside the ground, though, things turned nasty. When the Irish scored their first goal, hooligans situated in the upper tier of the west stand began ripping out seats and hurling them onto the heads of the Irish fans housed in the stand below them. Others invaded the pitch and, after further fighting, the game was abandoned after a mere twenty-seven minutes and the ground cleared of Irish fans. Hard-core English supporters stayed in the stadium fighting riot police for a further ninety minutes, leading to forty arrests and twenty serious injuries.

As the Irish police struggled to control the situation, things became quite nasty for the England fans who remained in the city. What follows was told to me by Steve of Bristol:

It seemed like every Irishman was out for blood that night. With most English lads packed off on ferries or to airports by the police, those of us who were left had a pretty rough night of it.

It wasn't long before we found ourselves in a row with a group of local lads. Although we stood and had a go, we had to back off in the end when more Irishmen started joining in. Luckily, this bouncer let us into a bar just round the corner. We'd only been in there about ten minutes when this fucking bicycle comes through the window! 'Course, first thing we do is steam outside and we find a fucking huge mob on the other side of the road. So we turn to go back into the bar only to find the bastards have locked the doors. In a situation like that, all you can do is front it up. Just as we're getting ourselves sorted, we hear sirens approaching. I tell you, I've never been so relieved to see a copper in my life.

Even as the cops were pouring out of their van, one of our lads walks out into the middle of the road and starts giving the Irish shit. Christ knows what he was thinking 'cause the first thing that happened was a copper whacked him one with this bloody great stick. It was fucking funny. Next thing we know, the police are putting us in cells for our own safety. It was a crazy night, but to be fair, you can kind of understand why the Irish were bit pissed off. I mean, we had fucked up their evening pretty well!

From a P.R. perspective, this was a massive success for the right wing. Even as the players were trooping off the pitch and the pictures were being broadcast around the world, an hysterical media, avoiding the obvious fact that the right-wing extremists they had spent years lambasting had actually been instrumental in starting the trouble, began pouring blame on the England fans. And, for the first time, the media began searching deeper into the background of the hooligans arrested. Life stories, families, and careers were dissected and explored in minute detail. The fact that some were in very well paying jobs astonished journalists who still clung to the belief that they were all simply brain-dead thugs who craved publicity. One of the men arrested on the pitch at Dublin, for example, was a company director. Another actually owned his own company.

Lurking on the horizon was Euro '96, the largest tournament England had staged since the 1966 World Cup. There had been calls to cancel the tournament, and after Chelsea fans were involved in violence in Belgium these became even louder. Thankfully, they were ignored, but the trouble at the end of the 1994–95 season has set a pattern. Media reports went into overdrive warning both the country and the game about the potential for trouble not just involving English lads but also those from abroad who were apparently looking to settle a few scores.

There had even been a resurgence of the Casual scene. Labels such as Burberry, Henri-Lloyd, Paul & Shark, CP Company, and of course Stone Island were now standard wear for anyone involved. Meanwhile, the police, desperate to foster the belief that they had the hooligans under control, began releasing press release after press release talking about arrest figures and intelligence reports and warning the hooligans that if they stepped out of line they would be hammered. For the firms, this was just the kind of challenge they relished, and rumors began to surface in the press of a so-called England superfirm involving the top boys from all the clubs in England. There were also rumors, spread in the media and by fans, that all the firms would link up and fight alongside each other. The rumors were all totally ridiculous and Euro '96 passed fairly peacefully. This was not because there weren't plenty of English lads ready for trouble—on occasion the center of London looked like a scene from *The Warriors*—but because only one nation brought any lads with them and that was Scotland. The rest seemingly bottled it.

The consequences of Euro '96 on hooliganism were twofold. First, the tournament had equipped the nation with a newfound love of the game, with many women discovering it for the first time, and second, the success of the police operation, albeit at a cost of more than $35 million, forced the hooligan groups into a major rethink.

By now it was accepted practice that the "normal" fans, or "scarfers" as they had become universally known, were not fair game and anyone dishing out any kind of violence to them was open to ridicule. As a result, it became standard practice at some clubs to track down visiting mobs when they came to town and then for one member of the home firm to visit them personally and suss out if they wanted to kick things off or not. If they didn't, for whatever reason, then they were simply left alone. If they were game, they were invited to a specific location at a specific time. This method allowed hooligan groups to avoid the police as well as keep innocent fans out of the action.

If the excitement around Euro '96 encouraged a new breed of fan it also attracted some old blood. Familiar faces began emerging on stands and terraces around the country. Returning to the game after years away and seemingly looking to recapture the buzz they'd gotten from being involved in trouble in the 1980s, many older hooligans began to get back into the action. They brought with them a willingness to fight that hadn't been seen at games in many years. At the same time, firms were beginning to devise even more ways to combat police interference in their activities. Increasingly, firms sent scouts into away grounds to suss out which areas were not covered by closed circuit TV, and if they found one suitable that's where they stood and, if possible, fought. Pagers also began to come into vogue as the police were beginning to become more and more suspicious of people using cell phones inside grounds.

As a result, trouble began to increase, and 1998 saw a huge upsurge in hooligan activity. In particular, attacks on officials began occurring with alarming frequency during the first few months of the year. The first came at Portsmouth when a Sheffield United fan jumped onto the pitch at Fratton Park and knocked out a lineman. In April, a supporter ran on to the pitch at Everton but was detained before he could get at the referee. On the very same day, Liverpool players had to wrestle fans to the ground as they attempted to attack the match official at Barnsley. Even worse, a Fulham fan was killed during disturbances at Gillingham. With the World Cup in France just weeks away, this was the worst possible news for the game. Already fears had been expressed about the possibility of trouble at the tournament involving England fans, and the police had been hard at work sorting out potential troublemakers. Indeed, just a week before the tragic death at Fulham, known English hooligans were prevented from entering Switzerland where England was playing a pre–World Cup warm-up game. The day after that, police raided the houses of twenty-nine men in Sunderland in an effort to prevent trouble in France that coming summer. Inevitably, the media got in on the act. More speculative and provocative headlines spewed out, and the government began warning of dire consequences should anyone travel without tickets. But people did travel without tickets and trouble did erupt, although not in the manner everyone expected.

The buildup to the tournament involved a huge anti-hooligan operation. Dawn raids were staged on the homes of numerous suspected ringleaders across England with several being filmed by invited TV news crews and shown on national television later that day.

Interestingly, in various briefings the FA's security adviser, Sir Brian Hayes, had asked the French police to recognize that the English fans could sometimes overreact to heavy-handed policing. In response, the French made it clear that they would go in heavy-handed only if things got really bad. Everyone was happy and confidence was high. Sadly, it was horribly misplaced.

The first signs of trouble came on the Saturday night when England fans who had settled into a bar in the old port area of Marseille spilled out onto the street and began showering motorists with bottles and glasses. They were driven back by more than a hundred policemen, some with dogs, but sporadic fighting continued for more than an hour.

The next day, there were more problems when a large group of local Tunisian immigrants who had been chanting and drinking outside a bar close to the center of town moved along the road toward a large crowd of Englishmen. Within minutes, the first bottle was thrown and pandemonium broke out. The police, who had been keeping their distance, moved in very quickly, firing at least five CS gas grenades into the English fans and forcing them away from the area. The media launched a scathing attack on the hooligans. Yet it was only a foretaste of what was to come.

On Monday morning, running battles broke out in the streets surrounding the old port, resulting in eighty England

fans being arrested, twenty-four injured, and one hospital-
ized after an attacker slashed an artery in his neck. There
was also serious disorder later on in the day when local
North Africans attacked England fans who were watching
the game on television screens that had been erected on
the beach. Despite the fact that the English support included many women and children, the French police just stood
by and watched events unfolding, becoming involved only
when the England fans decided to fight back.

The aftermath of France 1998 was one of close reflection
for the authorities. Prior to the tournament they had been convinced that they had done all they could to deal with the hooligan threat and had even gone on record saying that they knew
each and every potential troublemaker, how they were traveling, and where they were staying. Yet the morning after the
trouble in Marseille, shamefaced figures from both the FA and
the British police were forced to admit that they had no idea
who 99 percent of the people involved in the trouble were.

Yet for once, as fans returned from France telling stories
of how they had been brutalized by both the French locals
and the police, they began to receive a degree of sympathy
from the British public. However, if that sympathy was for
the game rather than the individual, it was sadly misplaced
for, as the new domestic season began, it quickly became
clear that hooliganism had returned in a big way.

As early as the August, twenty Norwich and QPR fans were involved in a bottle-throwing battle in a Norfolk pub. On September 19, people were arrested during the Swindon versus Oxford local derby, and that same month fighting broke out on a train carrying two hundred Manchester United and Coventry City fans to separate fixtures in London. Again in September, twenty Birmingham fans sprayed Norwich fans with CS gas and then attacked them with bar stools in a pub. In November, major trouble broke out on a London-to-Sheffield train that involved fans from Sheffield United, Chesterfield, and Nottingham Forest. This was just the tip of the iceberg as far as problems between fans were concerned. More worryingly, attacks on both players and team coaches were on the increase. By now it was becoming increasingly clear that the hooligans were making strong inroads back into the domestic game. The police, falling way behind in their efforts to contain the trouble, had even taken to targeting any lads wearing certain labels. A Stone Island sweater was a guaranteed way to attract the attentions of the police.

In November 1998, with one eye fixed firmly on a bid to host the 2006 World Cup, the British government announced a range of new legislation designed to counter the ever present threat of trouble around the national team. These included a plan to hand the police the power to ban suspected but not convicted hooligans from traveling to matches abroad simply on the word of a senior officer. Given that this circum-navigated the notion of "innocent until proven guilty," on which British law is based, this was an extremely risky idea, yet incredibly it received barely a whimper of comment.

For those involved in the scene, the document was mere-ly another challenge to be overcome. Many even expressed doubts (wrongly, as it turned out) that these laws would ever come on to the statute books. If the idea was to send a warn-ing to those intent on causing trouble, it fell sadly short. For in the quest to stay ahead in the contest with authority, the hooligans had discovered a new weapon, the Internet.

As 1999 arrived, there were approximately eight million subscribers to the Internet in Britain and many more people had access to it via their work. Given that right from the out-set a great deal of publicity had been given to the fact that the Internet could provide access to everything from hard-core pornography to lessons in nuclear-bomb building, it can hardly be surprising that fairly quickly people began to use it to spread news about soccer violence. Initially, these con-sisted of messages posted on some of the more unofficial club pages, but as people became more Internet-savvy web sites and message boards were set up dedicated to spread-ing information about upcoming hooligan activities. For ex-ample, the following was posted on a site the day after Bir-mingham City had visited Bristol City in April 1999:

Yesterday Birmingham city put on an impressive show
of force at Bristol City. About 10 minutes into the game to
the sound of "Zulu army" from the loyal nonce's already
in the ground, about 100–150 dressed up boys sauntered
into the seats wearing stone island, baseball hats and
sunglasses to avoid detection from the CCTV. Bristol had
a few boys out and both sides baited each other throughout the game but police had it well sussed with helicopter, dogs and horses—they have been well trained over
the years by Bristol's firm. After the game the Zulus were
looking to kick things off but were shadowed closely by
the police—more a show of force than any serious intent.

More worryingly, challenges also began to be thrown
down as did invites to "parties." A typical example of this is
the following:

Posted by P.N.E on May 07, 1999 at 12:56:44: STOP
PRESS; mob of 60/70 north end expected around Baker
St. Can you accommodate DAY OR NIGHT?

At the start of the 1999–2000 season, the press got hold
of this phenomenon for the first time when Millwall traveled
to Cardiff and serious trouble broke out. Somehow, the tabloids got the idea that the whole thing had been planned on

a certain Web site, and that as the trouble had been going on a running commentary had been posted for people who were not there. In fact, only a part of this is true. What did happen is that as soon as the entries were published, people using the Web began to build up the possibility of violence at the game (which was already likely given the history of the clubs involved). When it did kick off, a single descriptive posting was made online and the press picked up on it.

Because so much was made of this particular game in the press, the police went on a Web offensive. Messages began appearing on the main sites asking for specific details or offering information. Anyone who had spent time on these boards and knew the score realized quite quickly who was behind this, so bogus replies would be posted to anything suspicious. As a result, the majority of boards rapidly descended into chaos with as much as ninety-nine percent of the postings being pure bullshit.

Another problem for the police was that because of the increasing tabloid coverage of this new development, people suddenly began to believe that simply logging on to a site could lead to them being identified through their Internet service provider (ISP). To counter this, some of the more serious hooligans began using cybercafés and local libraries to send messages. Others simply stopped posting and reverted to more traditional methods of communication.

While all talk in the media was of the Internet, in the background other changes were taking place. To the amazement of many, the proposed anti-hooligan legislation had made it through the parliamentary process to become law. Among the first to discover just how powerful and far reaching these new powers would prove to be were a group of West Ham lads who were all set to travel to France for the final of the 1999 Anglo Italian Cup against Metz. Two days before they were due to leave, the group was contacted by the travel company it had booked to take them to the game and were told that the police had blocked the trip because there was insufficient time to check the identities of those who wanted to travel. The lads were naturally furious and, since they all had tickets for the game, they set out on a frantic search for an alternative modes of transportation. Sadly, not only were all aircraft heading in that direction full, but the trains were booked as well. The only alternative left was to drive. I did hear a rumor that their vehicles were turned back at the ports, although I have been unable to confirm this.

On the field, at least, soccer headed toward the new millennium in a confident and optimistic mood. The English Premiership league was firmly established as probably the most exciting in world soccer, and players from across the globe were flocking to England, attracted by the staggering wages offered and the opportunity to compete against the very best.

Even my beloved Watford had clawed its way into the top flight—if only for a single season—thanks to one of the most amazing playoff series I have ever known. Behind the euphoria lurked the same old problem with the violent minority.

The playoff series I just mentioned proves a case in point. The semifinals were a doubleheader against Birmingham City with the first game being played at Watford. We won this game 1–0 but the Birmingham hooligan firm, the Zulu Army, had hit the town en mass with a firm that I would estimate was made up of at least a thousand game lads. Not too shabby, considering Watford had only ever had a minor reputation in hooligan terms. Thankfully, trouble was small and largely involved problems in bars around the ground. Yet it was clear that the second leg would be a different matter entirely.

Now, at this point I should tell you that Birmingham's home ground is a formidable place to visit. The area can best be described as rough, and although the local people are warm and welcoming and the City fans capable of making a noise that will have your teeth rattling, their hooligans are fucking animals. There are also bloody thousands of them.

With the game meaning not simply a Wembley final appearance but a shot at getting into the English Premiership, the atmosphere was tense, to say the least, and we approached the ground with a great deal of trepidation.

I decided to drive with a carload of lads and found

myself being directed into a car park outside the ground. I quickly realized that we were the only Watford supporters in the car park, and the fact that we were in our best Casual gear marked us out immediately. The mood outside the ground was, to say the least, hostile. But thankfully there were so many Watford fans and policemen around that nothing untoward happened. After all, no one wanted to risk getting arrested and missing what was going to be one of the biggest games for either club in years.

In the event, Birmingham won the match 1–0, and with the aggregate scores tied it went into overtime. However, the mood was becoming increasingly ugly and every so often coins would come flying in our direction.

Incredibly, neither team scored during overtime and the match went into the dreaded penalty shoot-out. "Tense" doesn't even begin to describe what watching the shoot-out was like, especially when the five penalties allotted to each side were scored, meaning that the game went into sudden death. The feeling was indescribable. It was one of those games you hope you will always see, but when they come along you are so tense you expect a coronary at any second. At one point it was so bad that I turned and begged the bloke next to me for a cigarette. And I'd given up smoking in 1988.

Ten minutes later it was all over. Our keeper had pulled off an astonishing save and we had won 7–6. The place was going mental but as the players eventually trooped off the pitch and the thoughts of most people were turning to a Wembley final, those of us who knew what was what began to wonder what was waiting for us outside. We soon found out. The Zulus were fucking everywhere. Amazingly, they didn't attack. As I did, they looked so mentally drained—and in their case gutted—that they just didn't seem to have the inclination let alone the energy for a row. Within the hour we were out of Birmingham heading for home, still shocked at what we had seen on the playing field, never mind off it.

Despite our good luck that night, things had actually not been going well for a while. The latter part of 1999 had seen increasing hooliganism domestically, and concerns were being voiced about the potential for trouble at the forthcoming 2000 European championships, to be held in Belgium and Holland. Those concerns were heightened in November when the BBC broadcast a documentary allegedly exposing the hooligan group known as the Chelsea Headhunters.

Although presented in a sensationalist manner, the documentary merely took a large dose of stating the obvious and mixed it with a cocktail of half-truths and complete untruths to serve up something that was total bullshit. However, even as the BBC was indulging in its usual self-promotion by wheeling out the journalist involved onto every radio and TV show available, it received the best possible publicity when just three days after the broadcast a mob of around seven hundred hooligans from firms across England descended on Glasgow for the Scotland versus England Euro 2000 qualifier. In the event, a massive police operation involving 2,000 officers prevented the large-scale disorder many people had forecast, but there were still 170 arrests. The following week, the Scots descended on London for the return match. Again, there was a huge police operation, but fifty-six people were injured and thirty-nine arrested during clashes in the West End of London when a group of approximately fifty English lads attacked three hundred Scots in Trafalgar Square.

With the events of Glasgow and London fresh in the memory and Euro 2000 fast approaching, soccer's governing bodies moved into the new millennium in a nervous mood. Hooligan groups took their usual pre-tournament route as the groups once again began to adopt a lower profile to avoid anything that might prevent them traveling to watch England in the summer. By now, thanks largely to closed circuit TV, it was all but impossible to get a firm of any decent size into a town or onto the transport network without attracting the attention of the police, the consequence of which was that they would appear en mass and simply shadow you for the day.

On top of that, the policy of scrutinizing closed circuit TV footage of incidents and tracing everyone involved to make sure they were brought before the courts to receive an order banning them from attending soccer had all but stopped many lads from playing up at home altogether.

The Casual scene was also going through something of a change following the mid-1990s resurgence. As more and more people were cottoning on to the trend, some of the more active and elite Casual lads began to take the view that certain labels were becoming so mainstream that they were losing all credibility. Some even began removing the compass badge from Stone Island clothes so they were less obvious, although they left the two buttons on the sleeve to enable other lads to recognize them for who and what they were. Another consequence of this perceived elitism was that new and more exclusive labels began to appear on the scene, including Hackett, Prada, Duck & Cover, 6876, and One True Saxon.

Abroad, however, things continued along the same worrying path. Chelsea and Leeds fans were involved in serious disorder in France and Italy, respectively but this was simply a foretaste of what was to come. For within a matter of weeks, English soccer was dealt a blow that went way beyond anything we in this country had ever suffered before. Not for the first time it involved fans who had traveled abroad to watch their clubs being attacked with knives by local supporters. This time, instead of serious wounds, we had deaths.

CHAPTER SEVEN

International Violence

Within a matter of minutes, all sorts of things were flying through the air: metal chairs, lumps of wood, and signs that should have been directing people to various shops and bars.

Turkey has long been one of the favored destinations for English people on holiday. Almost a million people head for the country each year to enjoy the Mediterranean sunshine, cheap hotels, and the renowned hospitality of the Turkish people. For English soccer fans, however, a trip to this country is not always a great experience. To call Turkish supporters excitable would be something of an understatement; fanatical would be closer to the mark. This fanaticism often spills over into violence and Turkish soccer is well known for having a severe problem with hooliganism among its supporters.

On April 5, 2000, a small group of Leeds United fans was sitting in a bar in the middle of Istanbul. They were with a few hundred or so who had arrived in the city to watch their side play the first leg of a UEFA Cup semifinal against local side Galatasaray the following day. Although there had been reports of a few incidents of trouble in other bars, the group was confident of avoiding trouble and had settled down to have a few beers and enjoy the occasion. As the evening approached, some of the group realized that the bar had no TV and so, with Chelsea in action against the Spanish side Barcelona, they decided to head off to either find somewhere with a television or return to their hotels to watch the game there.

Unfortunately, as the first of them stepped out into the street, they came under attack from local hooligans. Within a matter of minutes, all sorts of things were flying through the air: metal chairs, lumps of wood, and signs that should have been directing people to various shops and bars. The Leeds lads from the bar retreated at first but quickly regrouped and fought back. Seemingly from nowhere, a TV news crew appeared and began filming everything. Then, to quote a mate of mine who was caught up in the middle of it all, "We started to see knives. Not the sort of knives that they stock down the local craft shops either. These things were more like swords. Certainly not something that anyone in their right mind would carry if they were just out for an evening stroll or quiet drink." The first of the stabbings happened almost immediately with one of the Leeds lads receiving serious slashing wounds to the backs of his legs and his hands.

Seeing this, the Leeds supporters ushered him back into the bar, where some of them tried to give him first aid. By the time the police finally began to take action—much of which involved trying to batter the Leeds fans senseless—numerous people had been badly wounded. Two English fans, Chris Loftus, who had been stabbed seventeen times, and Kevin Speight, who received six stab wounds, would die of their injuries.

Much of the incident was shown on TV. Included in many of the broadcasts was footage of one Leeds fan being hit repeatedly on the head by a Turkish policeman and kicked by Turkish hooligans while trying to give Chris Loftus mouth-to-mouth resuscitation. Even before the blood was dry on the streets, the Turkish media began inferring that the two lads had gotten what they deserved. Why else would English soccer fans have been in the city unless they had been looking to cause trouble?

Neither soccer's governing bodies nor the British government publicly condemned the actions of the Turkish hooligans and police, despite a consistent record of violence on the part of Turkish hooligans. In fact, the day before the murders, one of the most outspoken fans from the Turkish team

Fenerbahce was kidnapped by three supporters of a rival team who took him to a local picnic area and, using razor blades, sliced off his left ear, telling him to "feed this to the Fenerbahce pigs."

Like Italy, Holland, and Germany, Turkish soccer had always escaped sanction, while even the merest sniff of trouble involving the English game had attracted the full wrath of the head of European soccer Sepp Blatter. Ironically, those same fans now looked toward Blatter for action, but none was forthcoming. To say that there was a real sense of injustice among England's soccer supporters was an understatement. As a consequence, the hooligan community began talking about achieving its own form of justice, and the perfect opportunity readily presented itself. For having beaten Leeds, the Turkish team Galatasaray now faced another English club, Arsenal, in the UEFA Cup final, to be held in Denmark's capital city, Copenhagen.

With the potentially volatile UEFA Cup final fast approaching and Euro 2000 a matter of weeks away, the black cloud hanging over FA headquarters could be seen for miles. It was becoming increasingly clear to all that events in Denmark were going to have a major impact on what may or may not happen over the summer months. With the entire hooligan community—not just in England but across Europe—looking to Arsenal to avenge the murders of the two Leeds

United fans, Danish authorities feared that the large Turkish population who called Copenhagen home would unite behind Galatasaray and become involved in violence. They also voiced concerns that local hooligans would link with the English club and civil disturbances would result. Their fears were well founded.

Some six days before the final, it was reported that a group of Arsenal fans visited Copenhagen to familiarize themselves with the area and make contact with local lads. Two days later, police began erecting crowd control barriers in the cities main square.

The first clashes came the night before the game. Arsenal fans were drinking inside a disco when word spread that a group of Turks was lurking outside. The Londoners poured out, only to discover that the group was larger than expected. Undeterred, the Arsenal fans went for it, but in the resulting melee one received a serious stab wound. As more fighting broke out across the city, the police finally made an appearance. By the time things calmed down, seven people had been badly injured and ten were arrested.

The next day, a mob of Arsenal lads gathered in and around Rosie McGee's bar adjacent to Tivoli Gardens. On the other side of the square, hundreds of Turkish fans assembled, along with some local media. What started out as verbal abuse between the two sides soon escalated to the hurling of missiles. With no police presence and things getting uglier by the second, the Arsenal fans crossed the square and dealt out a battering. By the time it was all over, four people had been stabbed and sixty-four arrested. What follows is an account of events that day, supplied to me by Chris, an Arsenal fan from London:

The fucking Turks were on the other side of the square from us, and there were bloody hundreds of them, but not a policeman in sight. Even though we were well outnumbered, it was obvious it was going to kick off at some point. Pretty soon, the Turks started throwing stuff and that was it. Everyone just steamed across and went for it.

It was fucking mental. I've been in some scraps in my time, but this was something else. They were waving knives around, so we literally were fighting for our lives. There were lads using chairs, bottles, even a crush barrier to batter them. The funny thing was, when it was all over, we were the ones who got shit for using weapons!

Anyway, the police finally turned up and the Turks did a runner. Inevitably, we got the blame but so fucking what. We gave them a kicking and they deserved it. Wankers, the lot of them.

Inevitably, the blame was heaped on the English despite the fact that in the majority of incidents they had been forced to defend themselves in the face of overwhelming provocation and a lack of police protection. It is fair to say, however, that there was a sense of smug satisfaction among the hooligan community at what happened in Copenhagen. There have been many reports that in addition to Arsenal fans, there were a small number of representatives from Leeds United as well as various German, Danish, and even Swedish clubs involved in the fighting. Whatever the truth of the matter, the Turks certainly came off second best in a series of fights that, in a numerical sense, were more than weighted in their favor.

The media went into their usual frenzy, with the tabloids running story after story about the inevitability of trouble in the summer and the consequences that would have for the game. The police, meanwhile, went into overdrive. A series of dawn raids removed numerous lads from circulation, while anyone appearing in court for anything remotely linked to soccer was handed a banning order stopping them from attending games and forcing them to hand in their passports to prevent them traveling. On top of that, a list of more than one thousand names was passed to the Belgian and Dutch police with promises that if any were spotted they would be arrested and either deported or jailed immediately. That's assuming they actually made it out of the country. In terms of P.R., it appeared to be the last thing the game here needed, but in the hooligan community feelings were very different. Most English supporters simply took the lack of any real condemnation of the Turkish role in the trouble as confirmation that no matter what went on and where, if any English soccer fans were involved, they would be blamed.

Back in England, Millwall was involved in more trouble when their trip to Bristol City in March resulted in a semi-riot inside the ground with seats being ripped up by both home and away fans. Afterward, a group of around two hundred Millwall fans battled with riot police as they tried to get at rival supporters without success. With delicious irony, on the very same day, the 30,000-member England fan club, which had initially been set up by the FA to provide tickets and advice to traveling England supporters, was disbanded in a move designed to relaunch the English support with a more positive and hooligan-free image. Now anyone who wanted to follow England abroad was forced to reapply to the new organization, which allowed the police the opportunity to vet each and every application and decline those from anyone who might be a potential problem.

Soon thereafter, the world would be overtaken by a far more pressing worry when, on September 11, 2001, terrorists flew two airliners into the World Trade Center in New York. In Britain, a nation already suspicious of the Islamic religion, news reports of groups of British Muslims not only celebrating the attacks but advocating more outraged the population. Despite the fact that the vast majority of British Muslims were outraged by the attack as well, anti-Islamic feeling spread through large sections of England and it found a warm welcome among certain hooligan groups. Terraces begin to ring with taunts aimed at belittling the towns and cities of clubs with large ethnic populations, the best example being a resurgence of the old chant "Town full of Pakis, you're just a town full of Pakis." It was a worrying time for the antiracist organizations.

In October, Stoke City and Port Vale fans hit the headlines for all the wrong reasons when violence erupted at the Potteries derby. In all, eighty-four people were arrested during incidents that included a fight involving a hundred hooligans, some of whom were armed with iron bars and bricks. Trouble also occurred inside the ground, including a pitch invasion and a barrage of missiles being thrown onto the pitch. What was significant, however, were reports that a large group of Stoke fans was detained after the game en route to an area of the city that had been the scene of serious race riots earlier in the year. Of these fans, sixty were detained for chanting racial abuse.

As the game moved into the New Year and toward the 2002 World Cup in Japan and South Korea, the FA began showing increasing concern at the likelihood of trouble in the Far East. Banning orders were handed down freely to prevent hooligans from traveling to the game. The police also began refusing to release details of any trouble going on domestically, claiming that hooligans reveled in seeing their clubs featured in the press. Those familiar with the scene knew things were as out of control as ever, but any negative publicity would have undermined the P.R. drive being mounted by the police and the FA to convince the host nation that the World Cup in Japan would be trouble free. This was, to put too fine a point on it, bullshit. The next three months saw clashes involving numerous clubs. Among the litany of trouble were two incidents that were extremely significant albeit for different reasons.

The first involved Charlton and Southampton supporters who fought at Maze Hill railway station in South London. Although nothing major in hooligan terms, what marks this as important is the way that this so-called Battle of Maze Hill would later be used in dramatic fashion by both the police and the media. Fifteen or so Southampton fans got off the train at Maze Hill, to be met by twice the number of Charlton lads. Things kicked off immediately and lasted two or three minutes before the police arrived and the two groups did the off. With Japan on the horizon, the police latched on to the incident and, using closed circuit TV footage as well as mobile phone and computer records, managed to trace some of the men. Two years later, just ahead of Portugal 2004, seventeen of those involved were brought to trial.

What really captured media attention was the fact that one of the men, a teacher, hadn't even been present at Maze Hill, but was nevertheless sentenced to two years for his role in organizing the fight via the Internet. Immediately, the press began talking about hooliganism's cyber-subculture and suggested that this finally proved that soccer violence was indeed highly organized. For the police, the trials were a huge P.R. coup. The fact that Euro 2004 was so close allowed them to claim that all seventeen of the men imprisoned would have been heading for Portugal and so they had obviously removed a potential problem. The second event of note was perhaps the most significant in terms of the impact it had on hooligans at that time.

On May 2, 2002, South London saw what was described as some of the worst violence seen on the streets of the capital in living memory when Millwall fans rioted after their club's defeat to Birmingham City. At its height, almost a thousand Millwall fans spent more than an hour hurling bricks and paving slabs at police. Weapons including flares, fireworks, and even a chisel were used during the fighting. A number of cars were also set on fire.

So concerned were the police with the level of violence around the New Den, Millwall's stadium, that the Birmingham fans were kept locked inside the ground for over an hour before it was deemed safe enough for the Birmingham City players' coach to be escorted out. Only the arrival of reinforcements, which swelled police numbers to more than two hundred, managed to quell the trouble. The incident left forty-five officers injured, six of whom required hospital treatment for, among other things, a broken arm, a broken leg, and a broken foot. Significantly, every member of a twenty-one-strong Tactical Support Group unit were injured as were twenty-four out of thirty-six mounted policemen on duty. Three horses also suffered serious wounds, one of which proved nearly fatal.

The footage of this incident is absolutely terrifying and one can only wonder what it must have been like to have been in the middle of it. Indeed, after some months had passed, one of the policeman involved was interviewed and the poor guy was almost in tears, such had been his fear that night. The usual postmortem into the trouble included claims from furious senior police officers that the level of trouble was totally unacceptable and that they intended to sue Millwall soccer club for the cost of the operation and would be looking for compensation for officers injured on the night. However, this eventually came to nothing.

By now, all eyes were beginning to turn east, toward the 2002 World Cup in Japan and Korea. It is no exaggeration to say that the Japanese, force-fed by a crazed media with pictures of Millwall, Heysel, and Marseille, genuinely believed that Armageddon in the shape of English soccer fans was on the way. As if to confirm this, anti-riot exercises were staged using locals dressed in England shirts, and talk was of new technology such as net guns to fire at anyone who became involved in fighting. There were even companies making fortunes selling hooligan insurance to a terrified Japanese public.

In England, the wave of banning orders reached four figures while the media were going crazy reporting about hooligans using false passports, organized mobs heading for Thailand and Australia, and even stories of Japanese gangs threatening to take on the English hooligans. What no one realized, however, was that nothing was ever going to happen for one simple reason: Even if there had been lads traveling out looking for trouble, a claim that itself is debatable, there wasn't going to be anyone with whom they could fight. No other European company exports its hooligan problem, and there is no real culture of hooliganism in either Japan or South Korea. Not even the English can have a fight all by themselves. The tournament was a blast, and the English will long be remembered not for the trouble they brought with them but for the passion, noise, and color.

CHAPTER EIGHT

- -

Onward and Upward

Fighting began shortly after takeoff,
and blows were still being traded three
hours later when the plane landed.

An incident occurred in 2003 that has settled into hooligan folklore as one of the most audacious attacks ever staged by an organized group. Ironically, it received little or no coverage in the British press. Perhaps this is because it was simply so, well, unbelievable. The mob concerned was West Ham and their targets, their old sparring partners the Tottenham Hotspurs. With the game in midweek, the 7:45 p.m. kickoff gave the East London firm plenty of time to plan an attack. Around lunchtime, two large groups of about forty lads each headed off across London with the aim of hitting the Spurs at the Cockrell pub in Tottenham High Road. As the first of the two groups approached the pub, a mob of between thirty-five and forty-five Tottenham came pouring out of a side entrance and launched a barrage of missiles at the attackers. This offensive stopped West Ham in their tracks for a while, the second group of West Ham arrived, and together they forced the Tottenham lads to turn and run. Half of the Tottenham group made it back into the pub slamming the doors behind them, but in doing so they trapped their mates outside, who fled up the High Road.

The West Ham mob set about trying to force open the doors, but their efforts were wasted as the Cockrell is a former bank. They then laid siege to the windows, but these were also reinforced. With no way in they backed off.

At this point, the police finally arrived in the shape of two female officers, so West Ham headed off toward Northumberland Park where the Tactical Support Group finally got hold of them and arrested seventy-eight individuals. A good many lads managed to slip away as soon as the TSG appeared. More skirmishes took place throughout the evening, with at least two other pubs damaged. The final arrest total was ninety-three, the bulk of them West Ham. Nevertheless, this was a major victory for West Ham against their local and bitter rivals.

Questions remain as to how such a large group was able to travel across London without attracting attention from either the Metropolitan or the British Transport police.

There were even suggestions on the hooligan grapevine that the whole thing had been set up by the police in an attempt to gain sufficient evidence to smash the ICF once and for all. However, despite the large number of arrests, only a very few were ever convicted, which if nothing else highlighted the problems the police were having domestically. The events that night also showed just how difficult a job they faced in the coming months as Euro 2004 approached.

Luckily for them, the banning order system was proving increasingly effective with police adopting a "keep the problem in this country" approach and claiming that the 1,800 orders already in place would be supplemented by plenty more come the start of the tournament. At one stage there were twenty-eight separate forces conducting anti-hooligan operations targeting sixty-six clubs and more than six hundred specific targets. These ranged from infiltration and undercover operations to the ongoing review of closed circuit TV tapes of incidents in an effort to identify those who had been involved.

Even the Portuguese police remained quietly confident that the 50,000 Englishmen expected to arrive on their doorstep in the summer would be largely well behaved. These hopes didn't stop the Portuguese authorities from spending almost $23 million on a security operation that included, among other things, 150 new police cars and the first water cannons ever seen in Portugal.

The Portuguese also introduced border controls that allowed them to stop and detain anyone suspected of being a hooligan. Incredibly, the measures worked. The mood among England fans was light and friendly, and when they returned home after the sadly inevitable defeat in the quarter finals it was with their heads held high. With a few exceptions, they had done themselves and their country proud and for once they received glowing praise from all sides.

The same could not be said of those watching the tournament at home. The worst trouble witnessed as a result of the tournament took place back in England. For example, forty riot police and dog handlers battled to control hooligans in the center of Birmingham after the defeat to France, and in total, there were eight-three arrests that same night across the country. On the evening of England's defeat to Portugal, police on the island of Jersey were forced to break up a riot involving more than 1,400 people as disappointed locals turned their anger on one another. In Norfolk, a pub run by a Portuguese couple came under attack, while Exeter, Watford, and Croydon also saw trouble as people struggled to keep their emotions in check.

Perhaps inspired by the success of the measures in Portugal, police in the UK announced that they were going to take a nationwide zero tolerance approach to hooliganism. The key to this new approach was what they called their National Blueprint, which had been drawn up by the Association of Chief Police Officers and the Crown Prosecution Service to ensure consistency in the way that all forty-two police forces in England and Wales dealt with anyone charged with a soccer-related offense. Also included were measures imposing harsher penalties for less serious offenses such as smashing windows and even swearing. Combined with the legislation already in place, the police now had at their disposal some of the most draconian anti-hooligan laws to be found anywhere. In fact so stringent were they that magistrates had (and have) the power to apply a banning order to an individual if he plays up while watching a game on TV in a bar.

Finally, someone other than I began to voice concerns at the way things were going when the Soccer Supporters Federation came out with fears that some genuine fans might be unfairly punished. In response, a representative of Crown Prosecution Service was quoted as saying, "We are not talking about people celebrating and having a beer, we are talking about people who do that and then smash the bar up.'"

From that point on, the pressure on the hooligan scene was relentless, with forces up and down the country working with clubs to warn lads that if they stepped out of line they would get hammered. Equally, intelligence prevented all kinds of prearranged meetings between rival mobs. To an extent, this suppression worked. Certainly instances of large-scale disorder tailed off dramatically, but in some ways these tactics simply played into the hands of those involved. The measures provided many hooligans with an excuse to simply take a step back for a while in the hope that they would be able to travel to Germany for the 2006 World Cup the following summer.

The game moved into 2006 with all eyes cast nervously in the direction of Germany and the forthcoming World Cup, and there was a more positive feel to things where England fans were concerned. Even the British embassy in Berlin exuded quiet confidence, pointing out that only five English fans had been arrested at the past seven international matches. For the police, the usual pre-tournament round of dawn raids and anti-hooligan P.R. began in earnest. On top of that, banning orders were being handed out like confetti, and by the time the tournament arrived, more than 3,200 were in place. With that number of known or suspected hooligans taken out of the equation, coupled with a huge security operation at ports and airports to spot and detain anyone who had slipped through the net, it should come as no surprise to discover that, at least as far as the English were concerned, it worked. Almost.

The first major trouble erupted when English and German hooligans fought in Frankfurt after the opening matches, resulting in twenty arrests. A further 240 German hooligans were arrested in Dortmund after clashes with police on the day of the home nation's tie with Poland, a game many had cited as the key flashpoint of the entire tournament. Just days later, English and German fans clashed twice in Stuttgart, resulting in three hundred arrests while a further eighty were arrested after violence following the semifinal defeat to Portugal.

Despite the seemingly high number of hooligan-related arrests, the authorities deemed the tournament a major success and the England fans were once again widely praised for their behavior. But not for the first time, things were slightly different at home. On the night the nation's soccer team crashed out of the tournament, fans rioted the length and breadth of England. So serious did it become that at one point every single jail cell in a number of towns and cities was full.

As the 2006–2007 domestic season opened, the seemingly endless cycle of hooliganism began again. More often than not, when hooliganism did make the newspapers, it was for reasons that had nothing to do with violence. The first occasion came when the police announced that they would be testing a new weapon in the ongoing battle, the head-cam, a small camera that could be fitted to a policemen's helmet to capture images that might provide evidence in court at a later date. In a country that has more closed circuit TV cameras covering its population than any other nation on the planet, the head-cam received widespread condemnation as a step too far. As usual, the fact that it was linked to the battle against soccer violence allowed the authorities to force it through into legal use.

The second occasion was even more laughable. Designer clothing labels had long been associated with the soccer hooliganism and some such as Stone Island had actually been formed on the back of the Casual culture. This was never truer of any label than it has been of Burberry, for years the favored label of hooligans everywhere. Indeed, it has been argued that Burberry was saved from obscurity by the Casuals. The company, however, had battled hard to disassociate itself from soccer, and when police launched an operation to target hooligans at Millwall under the banner of Operation Burberry, the company was less than pleased and even threatened legal action.

While trouble continued to dog the domestic game both at home and on European excursions, things had changed on the international scene thanks largely to years of sustained police action coupled with sterling efforts by the fans themselves. Indeed, it is fair to say that the demographic shift in the English support from "hooligan" to "fan" was now all but complete. The problem was, no one had bothered to tell the rest of the world. Whenever English fans traveled abroad, they were inevitably confronted by either groups of local hooligans looking to kick off trouble to enhance their own reputations or battalions of riot-gear- equipped policemen. Never was this more evident than when the team traveled in October 2006 to Croatia, a country that has a major hooligan problem of its own. The night prior to the game saw a minor skirmish involving fewer than thirty fans, but the following day, as fans waited to enter the stadium, the police simply waded in and batoned anyone and everyone for what was seemingly no reason. The condemnation against the police was swift, vocal, and just but, more important, this time it came from all sides, including the press and the game's authorities. Bizarrely, in a move that was met with something approaching total outrage in England, the game's European governing bodies charged both England and Croatia for their parts in the trouble.

Hooliganism hit the headlines again in November when a British Airways jet was forced to make an emergency landing in London when fans of CSKA Moscow, en route to a champions league tie against London club Arsenal, began fighting among themselves before turning on cabin crew, who were unable to control them. According to reports, the fighting began shortly after takeoff, and blows were still being traded three hours later when the plane landed.

Increasingly, the eyes of the European authorities turned away from England as hooliganism on the continent became big news. In January, a group of AC Milan Ultra was arrested when it was alleged that they had been trying to blackmail the club with threats to disrupt matches. In France, a twenty-five-year-old alleged member of the notorious right-wing hooligan group the Boulogne Boys was shot and killed by a policeman who came under attack as he tried to detain a Jewish supporter of the Israeli team Hapoel Tel Aviv. Things really came to a head when an Italian policeman was killed after being struck by fireworks during riots at the Sicilian derby between Catania and Palermo.

As news of the death spread around the world, the Italian authorities suspended all soccer in the country, some 10,000 matches. Incredible though it might seem for a nation that has been dogged by the violent Ultra culture for decades, Italy had only limited powers to deal with soccer hooliganism. English fans had long felt that the Italian fans had been treated with astonishing leniency by the game's European governing bodies. This light-handed approach, however, finally began to change when the Italian government announced that it would be introducing tough new measures, including barring soccer fans from stadiums where security requirements where not met, a ban on the block sale of tickets to away fans, and a ban on financial or working relationships between clubs and fan associations. These new measures were not universally welcomed. One Italian club chairman accused the government of creating a fascist climate around the game while others warned that clubs simply would not accept the new laws and more trouble would result. Another nation that seemed to have finally had enough was Germany, which, following a riot involving eight hundred hooligans in Saxony, threatened to ban soccer altogether. Ultimately, though, only games in the region were suspended.

Events elsewhere had also taken the English media's eye off of the continuing domestic problem but that was to change in March when, once again, it was dragged back onto the front pages. On March 11, 2007, a group of Chelsea fans was drinking outside the White Horse pub in Parsons Green, West London. The bar is a well-known drinking place for Chelsea lads on match days, and having beaten local rivals Tottenham Hotspurs in a cup tie earlier in the day, Chelsea packed the place.

Suddenly, a shout went up and a group of Tottenham fans appeared armed with a variety of weapons, including knives, baseball bats, wooden clubs embedded with nails, and hockey sticks. In the resulting riot, at least ten people were stabbed before dozens of police officers, including vans of riot police that had been on standby, and a police helicopter scrambled to the scene. After struggling for more than an hour to regain control, police arrested thirty-four men, including seven who were taken to the hospital suffering from stab wounds and head injuries.

It was a highly organized attack, and when rumors began to surface that it had been organized on the Internet, the press went crazy. Just a few weeks later, three Manchester United fans were stabbed during clashes with both police and members of the Roma Ultra in Italy ahead of a champions league tie with Roma, and the following evening Tottenham's trip to Spain was marred by violence inside and outside the stadium.

Sadly, the footage from both incidents was broadcast around the world and with the blame for both laid fairly— and correctly—at the feet of the local police and supporters, all attention became focused on the return leg of the Manchester tie a week later where fears of revenge attacks by the English were very real.

Things weren't helped by news that the members of Roma Ultra had secured a huge number of tickets and made it known that they would be coming to England en masse. In the event, a huge police operation kept clashes to a minimum, with the worst one taking place on the stadium forecourt as police struggled to keep the two sets of fans apart. Though the incident received widespread coverage, it was overshadowed by events on the pitch, for Manchester United delivered what will go down in history as one of the great team performances by demolishing Roma 7–1.

In spite of the strides made to deal with the hooligan menace on the international stage, the hooligan problem continues to dog the English domestic game. And make no mistake, things will get worse before they get better.

AFTERWORD

Next Stop America?

For those of us in countries where soccer is fully entrenched in sports culture, what happens in the stands during the game, be it humor, abuse, or even hooliganism, has always been an important and integral part of the match day experience. For example, while in Russia recently, I attended a game between two of the big Moscow clubs, Spartak and Locomotive, and so spectacular was the crowd in terms of the singing, chanting, and flag waving that I spent almost the whole game watching them, not the players. Can you imagine doing that at a baseball game in the United States? NFL, basketball, and even NASCAR crowds might be noisy and passionate, but when was the last time you heard an entire stadium singing in unison? The opportunity to witness this type of spectacle in the United States might not be that far away. The appearance of so many American soccer fans at the 2006 World Cup proved that the popularity of the game is on the rise in the United States, and all but banished the long-held impression of soccer as being the domain only of the "soccer mom."

Already, across the United States, dedicated and enthusiastic soccer fans are banding together to form organized groups. With names like La Barra Brava (DC United), Section 8 (Chicago Fire), Raging Bull Nation (Red Bull New York), and the Galaxians (LA Galaxy), these groups have begun to create the kind of charged atmosphere inside stadiums that soccer fans the world over enjoy week in and week out. Fans sing songs, wave banners, and generally have a blast as they provide as much vocal and visible support for their teams as they possibly can.

So far, the fledgling soccer-fan culture in America has largely been devoid of hooliganism. Yet I have no doubt that, if the game sits back and waits to see what happens, you will almost certainly see soccer violence take hold in America. In my mind, there are only two reasons why hooliganism hasn't begun with any real force already. The first is distance. Compared to England, for example, which is a relatively small island, the United States is vast. Visiting fans from very far away are rare at games. Hence you have no real opportunity to develop the extended interfan rivalries we have. That, however, is already changing. Glance at any MLS fan site and you'll see details for forthcoming road trips, some cross-country. The numbers involved are minuscule compared to what we see in England, and there is certainly no evidence to suggest that those who make these trips are anything other than regular fans, but this type of organized movement around the country could devolve into something else entirely. The second and most important reason the United States has been spared hooliganism so far is simply that the country is starting with a pretty clean slate. There is none of the history and mob rivalry that underlies hooligan culture in the UK.

The existence of this cultural vacuum on American terraces is, however, actually one of the key reasons why hooliganism may well overcome these obstacles and take root in America. The increased popularity of soccer in the United States has been partially fueled by the growth in fans from a number of ethnic-minority communities who live in the country. This is often reflected in the style of fan support adopted by the various groups. La Barra Brava, for example, follow the South American style of supporting with rhythmic drums, streamers, and chanting while groups such as the Screaming Eagles, who follow DC United appear to have embraced a more European approach with a spontaneous and humorous feel to their songs.

While the majority of these groups promote an "all are welcome" policy in terms of membership, the reality is that some have become almost ethnically exclusive in their makeup. This is a potentially serious problem. Restricting membership to one ethnicity can lead to only one thing: trouble. The terraces have, after all, been the traditional place for citizens to share their opinions and vent their frustrations, and they can provide fertile ground for political extremism.

The formation of separatist fan groups isn't the only thing that should be of concern to the game in the United States. There is a far greater menace lurking and it isn't on the terraces; it's on the street. In a nation where youth culture appears to be dominated by hip-hop, there are teenagers and twenty-somethings who have no interest in this scene and, as a consequence, are looking for something to embrace as their own. Could that particular void be filled by the cult of the Casual? Of course it could.

It has everything anyone could ever want. Clothes, sport, politics—even anarchy. Throw in the facts that it has no hard-and-fast affiliations with any form of music and is a gang culture in all but name and is something fresh and new —at least in the US—and you have the perfect scene. And it doesn't demand the kind of overt exhibitionism associated with skinhead or punk. In short, Casual could finally make it cool to be young, white, and urban.

Think I'm joking? Well, think again. Since 1996 I've written twelve books on the subject of hooliganism and they've all found a dedicated and very enthusiastic following in the United States. Furthermore, the Web is full of US-based sites dedicated to my movie, *Green Street Hooligans,* and, just as I feared, in most cases they entirely miss the point I wanted to make. Rather than talk about the violent and ultimately destructive lifestyle, they focus on the clothes and the actors. I don't know exactly how many of these individuals have started aping the characters by going to games wearing all the gear and talking the talk, but I know from the amount of mail I receive that plenty have. How long will it be before some of them begin to adopt some of the less attractive traits of the scene? The elitism? Arrogance? Dislike and distrust of other groups even from the same club? The violence?

In fact, if you study the trouble at the 2006 season opener between Red Bull New York and their rivals DC, which, thanks to someone's handheld camera, appeared on YouTube within hours, the parallels with the game in England are obvious, and not just in how the trouble unfolded but in the way the participants looked and acted. Taunting inside the ground, the odd punch thrown, people being hit by missiles, and even a confrontation in the car park after the game involving a group of skinheads—all reminiscent of England in the 1980s when hooliganism was at its height. Coincidence? Surely not.

The consequence of this violence will be that the fans of these two clubs now have a history and there is a score to settle. Sound familiar? It should, because that, my friends, is how hooliganism develops. You think that as aggression among fans becomes a regular feature at the Gillette Stadium or Toyota Park it won't soon filter down to the colleges and the schools? Think again. It happens here in England every weekend. The semipro and even amateur game is a hotbed of hooligan activity—often involving lads banned from attending professional games—and it happens almost everywhere the game is played as well. Sadly, the actual violence isn't the only problem; there is everything else that goes with it.

Here in England we are so used to the impact of hooliganism on the culture that we no longer even notice the legions of riot police or the numerous security cameras that track our every move when we attend games. Nor do we think about the fact that fans are always segregated or that tickets for traveling fans are often heavily restricted and closely controlled. Do you really want that in the United States?

If the MLS is clever, it will realize that the key to what happens next lies with the fans themselves. Given the help and support of the teams, the existing supporter groups will continue to develop a positive fan culture, which will not only enhance soccer but become something that other fans and sponsors will clamor to be a part of. Most important, as the example of the England national side has proven, the best defense against hooliganism is the majority of law-abiding fans. They must be actively encouraged to police themselves. Basic peer pressure is the key. If a potential problem rears its head, and everyone tells the perpetrators to behave or fuck off, problems will start to go away.

If—and it's a big if—the MLS does decide that it isn't going to sit back and let hooliganism take over soccer as both the European and South American games have, then it must understand that, far from being a potential problem, the fans are actually the game's biggest asset. If this can be understood then soccer may they have a shot at finally pushing itself forward to the point where it can legitimately be thought of as comparable to the NFL, the NBA, MLB, and NASCAR. Who knows? Maybe one day you'll even begin to call the game football.

APPENDIX: MOB BREAKDOWN

Team	Associated Hooligan Firms
Arsenal	Gooners
Aston Villa	Villa Youth
	Steamers
Barnsley	Five-O
	Inner City Tykes
Birmingham City	Zulu Army
Blackburn Rovers	Blackburn Youth
Blackpool	BRS (Bison Riot Squad)
	Seaside Mafia
	The Mob
Bolton Wanderers	Billy Whizz Fan Club
	Mongoose Cuckoo Boys
	Tonge Moor Slashers
	The Omega

Bradford City	The Ointment
Brighton	Headhunters
	West Streeters
Bristol City	Inner City Robins
	East End
Bristol Rovers	The Gas
	The Tote
	The Pirates
Burnley	SS (Suicide Squad)
Bury	The Interchange Squad
Cambridge United	Cambridge Casuals
	Pringle Boys
Cardiff City	Soul Crew
	PVM (Pure Violence Mob)
	Dirty 30
	D Firm
	Valley Commandoes
	The Young Boys
	B Troop
	The Motley Crew

Carlisle United	BCF (Border City Firm)
	BSC (Benders Service Crew)
Charlton Athletic	B Mob
Chelsea	Headhunters
	Shed Boot Boys
	North Stand Boys
	Pringle Boys
	APF (Anti Personnel Firm)
Chesterfield	CBS (Chesterfield Bastard Squad)
Colchester United	The Barsiders
Coventry City	The Legion
	The Coventry Casuals
Crewe Alexandra	RTF (Rail Town Firm)
Crystal Palace	Naughty 40
	Whitehorse Boys
	Nifty Fifty
Darlington	Darlington Casuals
	Bank Top 200
	The Gaffa
	Under 5s
	The Townies

Derby County	DLF (Derby Lunatic Fringe)
	C Seats
	C Stand
Doncaster Rovers	DDR (Doncaster Defence Regiment)
Everton	Scallies
Exeter City	Sly Crew
City Hit Squad	
Fulham	TVT (Thames Valley Travellers)
Grimsby Town	CBP (Cleethorpes Beach Patrol)
Halifax Town	The Casuals
Huddersfield Town	HYC (Huddersfield Young Casuals)
Hull City	City Casuals
	City Psychos
Ipswich Town	IPS (Ipswich Protection Squad)
Leeds United	Service Crew
	YRA (Yorkshire Republican Army)
Leicester City	Baby Squad
Leyton Orient	OTF (Orient Terrace Firm)

Lincoln City	LTE (Lincoln Transit Elite)
Liverpool	Huyton Baddies
	The Scallies
Luton Town	Migs (Men in Gear)
	BPYP (Bury Park Youth Posse)
Manchester City	Guv'nors
	Maine Line Service Crew
	The Borg Elite
	Moston Cool Cats
	Motorway Crew
Manchester United	Cockney Reds
	Inter City Jibbers
	Red Army
	MIB (Men in Black)
Mansfield Town	The Carrot Crew
	MSE (Mansfield Shaddy Express)
Middlesborough	Frontline
Millwall	The Half-Way Liners
	F Troop
	The Treatment
	Bushwhackers

Newcastle United	Gremlins
	NME (Newcastle Mainline Express)
	Bender Crew
Northampton Town	NAT (Northampton Affray Team)
Norwich City	Barclay Boot Boys
	NHS (Norwich Hit Squad)
	ETC (Executive Travel Club)
Notts County	The Bullwell Crew
	Roadside Casuals
Nottingham Forest	Red Dogs
	Naughty Forty
	Executive Crew
Oldham Athletic	Fine Young Casuals
Peterborough United	PTC (Peterborough Terrace Crew)
Plymouth Argyle	TCE (The Central Element)
	Devonport Boys
Portsmouth	657 Crew
Port Vale	VLF (Vale Lunatic Fringe)
Preston NE	Leyland Boys

QPR	Ladbroke Grove Mob
	Fila Mob
Reading	Berkshire Boot Boys
Rotherham United	Rotherham Casuals
	Section 5
Scunthorpe United	The Ironclad
Sheffield United	BBC (Blades Business Crew)
	BBA (Bramall Barmy Army)
Sheffield Weds	OCS (Owls Crime Squad)
	Inter-City Owls
Shrewsbury Town	EBF (English Border Front)
Southampton	The Ugliest
	Inside Crew
	Suburban Casuals
Southend United	CS Crew
Stoke City	Naughty 40
Stockport County	The Company
	Hit Squad

Sunderland	Seaburn Casuals
	Boss Lads
	Vauxies
	The Redskins
Swansea City	Swansea Jacks
	Jack Army
	Jack Casuals
	Stone Island Casuals
Swindon Town	Gussethunters
	Southsiders
	South Ciders
	Town Enders
	SSC (South Side Crew)
Torquay United	Torquay Youth
Tottenham Hotspur	Yiddos
	N17s
	Tottenham Casuals
	The Paxton Boys
Tranmere Rovers	TSB (Tranmere Stanley Boys)
Walsall	SPG (Special Patrol Group)
	Barmy Army

Watford	Category C
	TWM (The Watford Men)
	DDF
	Watford Youth
West Brom	Section Five
West Ham United	ICF (Inter City Firm)
	Under 5s
	Mile End Mob
Wigan Athletic	The Goon Squad
Wolverhampton	Subway Army
	Bridge Boys
Wrexham	Frontline
York City	YNS (York Nomad Society)

If you would like to learn more about Dougie Brimson, please visit www.brimson.net.